The Everyday Girls Guide
to Living in Truth, Self-Love, and Acceptance

Co-Authors
Crystal D Life
Natalie Smith
Carolyn Hobdey
Michelina Cusano
Meg Scott
Laura Dempsey
Eliana Keen
Lesley Fraser
Hillary Sepulveda Brown
Kim Garden
Lisa King
Judy Prokopiak
Kym Laube
Mandy Monson
Renae Peterson
Tierra Womack, MBA
Randi Willhite
Kathryn Van Der Steege
Iona Russell

BALBOA.PRESS
A DIVISION OF HAY HOUSE

Balboa Press books may be ordered through booksellers or by contacting:

Balboa Press
A Division of Hay House
1663 Liberty Drive
Bloomington, IN 47403
www.balboapress.co.uk
UK TFN: 0800 0148647 (Toll Free inside the UK)
UK Local: (02) 0369 56325 (+44 20 3695 6325 from outside the UK)

Because of the dynamic nature of the Internet, any web addresses or links contained in
this book may have changed since publication and may no longer be valid. The views
expressed in this work are solely those of the author and do not necessarily reflect the
views of the publisher, and the publisher hereby disclaims any responsibility for them.

The author of this book does not dispense medical advice or prescribe the use
of any technique as a form of treatment for physical, emotional, or medical
problems without the advice of a physician, either directly or indirectly. The
intent of the author is only to offer information of a general nature to help you
in your quest for emotional and spiritual well-being. In the event you use any
of the information in this book for yourself, which is your constitutional right,
the author and the publisher assume no responsibility for your actions.

Any people depicted in stock imagery provided by Getty Images are
models, and such images are being used for illustrative purposes only.
Certain stock imagery © Getty Images.

Print information available on the last page.

ISBN: 978-1-9822-8441-1 (sc)
ISBN: 978-1-9822-8442-8 (e)

Balboa Press rev. date: 10/13/2021

CONTENTS

INTRODUCTION

Welcome to The Everyday Girls Guide to Living in Truth. Self-Love, and Acceptance!
This book is your perfect source of understanding, compassion, and support, as you navigate this exciting and sometimes daunting chapter teen life.

Including guidance and wisdom from 19 incredible teen girl mentors from around the world, each chapter will support you in different areas of your life.

At the end of each chapter, you will be guided to explore, journal, contemplate what has been shared and how you can see this play out in your life.

It is not a 'how to' it is a 'how do YOU want life to be'

As a teen girl, we are passionate about you feeling empowered and confident as you go on your journey at this stage of your life and this book will support you through that!

So, enjoy this exploration, take what you feel resonates, stand in your awesome power, embrace all of who you are and most of all ENJOY this part of life, enjoy and embrace every moment!

Tons of Love,

Leanne
Founder – She Speaks Media

This book is brought to you by She Speaks Media, a platform dedicated to creating resources that spark transformation in women and teen girls around the world.

CHAPTER ONE

Words Have Power

Words have POWER. Positive or negative. Spoken to you or by you. Aimed at other people or yourself.

There is a saying.

'Sticks and stones may break your bones, but words will never hurt you'.

Something that parents would say to their children if other kids spoke unkind words to them.

But I discovered that no matter how well-intentioned these words of comfort were, the statement was just not true.

If, when you are growing up, the only words you hear about yourself are negative; you are ugly, you are fat, you are dumb, etc. Then the truth is, words *do* hurt. Those words shape your reality and you become unable to see your true worth. You begin to believe the negative words and phrases replaying over and over in your head.

However, I have news for you. You have a choice to believe them or not. You need to know that you are ENOUGH!

These days, as a teen girl, you face huge pressure. As amazing as social media can be, if you are not secure in who you are, you may be vulnerable to the opinions of others. You will base your worth on how many likes you receive on a picture or video you have posted. Or on how many followers you have on your social media platforms.

In reality, those things are superficial, and your self-worth should NEVER be based on something so inconsequential.

There is a wonderful video that went viral on YouTube and, has since been turned into a meme for all the world to see. I believe every young girl should adopt it as their mantra. The video is of a young girl, around five or six. She is holding a mug and she says: 'I don't care if you don't like me, I LOVE me! WOW! Imagine being that confident at such a young age. She knows that her worth is not determined by the opinions of others but is all about how she feels about herself.

What do you think would happen if you adopted the same attitude? What if you posted a picture on your social media and only got 10 likes as opposed to 100? Would you still like the picture, or would you take it down? What would happen if you had a powerful message, filled with hope and compassion, that could impact someone's life for the better? And you posted it but only received five likes. Would you keep it up or take it down?

Girls grow up reading fairy tales, that tell stories of beautiful, kind girls who overcome many hurdles before finding their prince and living happily ever after. Beauty and the Beast, Cinderella, Sleeping Beauty and Snow White and many more.

Let's look at Snow White. The wicked stepmother was haunted and obsessed with being the fairest in the land. So much so that she needed constant reassurance from the person in the mirror. She would ask the same thing over and over.

'Mirror, mirror on the wall. Who is the fairest of them all?"

I always wondered how the story would have turned out if the wicked stepmother was not constantly seeking validation from everyone else. Why was it so important to her that others saw her as the fairest? instead of her seeing herself in that way. What a different story would have played out. My, how the tables could have turned if she saw in herself what she longed for others to see. I wonder what negative self-talk she used, that made her compare herself to Snow White and find herself wanting?

What do *you* say when you look in the mirror? Are you longing to be your favorite rapper; songwriter; or famous model or even the most popular girl in school? Or are you like the wicked stepmother? Seeking the validation of others, instead of looking in the mirror and telling yourself that YOU are ALL that you need to be. That you like who you are, just the way you are. When you can do that, you have the power to control your own worth, without giving that power to anyone else. Take your power back and remember you do not need to seek approval from anyone.

In 2016, Deshauna Barber won the title Miss USA 2016. In an interview, she talked about her life growing up and her journey to winning the crown. She shared that just like many other girls she was terribly bullied in high school. She recalled how she would be called skinny. And monkey because her arms and feet were so long. She had such low self-esteem, she decided early on that she would join the military. But one day at the age of 19, someone saw something in her that she did not see in herself. 6 years later she became Miss USA. Just as her pageant coach had told her she would, that day in the Target store.

My story was similar. I developed much faster than other girls, so I was teased and called "titty city" I was taunted because of the complexion of my skin. I was so invested in what other people thought of me that I began to believe what they said, and it began to destroy the image I had of myself.

I was like the wicked stepmother in Snow White. Looking in the mirror as a young girl, I saw more things wrong with me than right. In my eyes. Compared to others, I had nothing going for me. Ultimately, that belief became my downfall. I was too short; my skin was not right; my hair was not the perfect texture and my fashion sense sucked.

The crazy thing is – no one ever saw this side of me. Because I wore an invisible mask that hid the real me. Others assumed that because my confidence in my abilities was so high that they never paid any attention to me. So, I lurked in the background, trying desperately not to be seen.

In my junior year of college, all of that changed when I met my dear friend Leslie. Leslie had incredible self-esteem. She was magnetic and you could not help but be drawn to her aura. I recall a conversation, when one of our friends laughingly said to Leslie; 'You are so conceited' Without blinking, Leslie replied, 'No, I'm not conceited, but I am convinced. There's a difference!'

That statement completely changed the way I looked at myself. From that moment, Leslie and I embarked on a journey that changed my life. Years later I shared with her that she was pivotal in helping me re-create myself. She gave me the confidence to step up, to stop talking myself down and allow my light to shine.

Leslie and I became the best of friends and we stayed roommates until the day I graduated college.

We lost contact over the years, but I never forgot how she helped me see myself for who I was, simply by being who she was. Discovering who I was, became easier for me because I was no longer around the people I grew up with. The people who were part of the reason I had such low self-esteem.

I began journaling and placed all my fears, my preconceived inadequacies down on paper. Later on, I learned to identify my strengths. So that every time negative thoughts entered my mind, I would reject them and focus on my strengths.

I began writing an affirmation a day, to remind me of how worthy I was in case one of those negative thoughts crept up on me. Since then, I have purposefully made it my mission to be around other people who will push me to greatness. People who see in me that which I cannot see in myself.

Nowadays I intentionally affirm others because I never want anyone to feel the way I did. To not understand their true value.

Years ago, I remember attending a conference to equip youth leaders like me with tools to use while ministering to the youth. One speaker ended his lecture by holding a crisp $100 bill in his hands. He asked the group; 'Who would like this $100 bill'.

Lots of hands shot up in the room. Then he crumpled the $100 bill up in his hands and asked the group again; "How about now, do you still want it?'

More hands went up! They still wanted it.

Then the speaker threw the crumpled bill into a nearby trash can. He asked again 'Do you still want the $100?'

Even more engaged, everyone stood, clapped, and screamed 'YES!'

The speaker took the $100 bill out of the trash can and smoothed it out. He ended his lecture by saying; 'No matter what I put this $100 bill through, it never loses its value. Regardless of what we may experience on this journey called life, no matter how many mistakes we make, no matter who does not see our value, YOU still hold value.'

Remember, it is really not about the number of likes, or how many followers you have on social media. You are still valuable. If other people do not see your worth, make sure you do.

If you pass a mirror and see your reflection, you will not need to ask, 'Who is the fairest of them all?' Because you already will know that YOU are.

As my college friend taught me, it is not that you are showing arrogance, you are simply convinced!

I have a few tips for you.

- Practice self-love always by focusing on your strengths and not your weaknesses.
- Eliminate negative self-talk. When a negative thought creeps into your mind, immediately replace it with a positive thought!

- At all costs, surround yourself with positive people, that will affirm you as much as you affirm them.
- Remember to SMILE – you got this!

Go forth and be all that you have been created to be.

CHAPTER TWO

I see you

I want to start my chapter in gratitude!

Gratitude to you for taking the time to read these words. Your time is precious but here you are CHOOSING to read this book. Pause for a moment and think about that - you could be doing anything you want to do right now, feel proud of yourself for taking the time to learn and grow!

This book is the book that I wish I had read as a teen. I am hoping that you do not just read the chapters, but that you genuinely start to implement the lessons offered into your life.

Teens, I see you! I want to start by acknowledging that I know life as a teen can be a tricky thing to navigate. You are learning about putting boundaries in place with parents and peers and making decisions about your future. But at the same time, you are trying to find a balance between dealing with your responsibilities and having lots of freedom and fun!

It is a time of self-expression and discovering your true identity. Figuring out who that beautiful young woman is, deep in her core.

If there was one thing that I wished that I had learned when I was younger, it is this;

'Life is just like a game, and we have to learn to play it'

Let me explain what I mean by that. Imagine a computer game; you are at the starting line in a little car and your goal is to get to the end of this level.

Ready. Get set. GOOOOOO!

You start great and it is easy. There are only a few players on this level... but then watch out! You see a banana skin...phew! You avoided it! Then you see some coins to collect, 'ding, ding, ding' feeling good! You have been so happy collecting the coins, you did not see the banana skin. Wah! Wah! Wah! One life lost.

You start again, this time you remember where the banana skins are, so you do not slip up. You keep going and manage to avoid the things that are trying to catch you out. You are learning all of the LESSONS so quickly!

Oh no! Someone throws something at you to catch you out, BOOM! Another life gone.

You finally get near the end of the level and you know what is coming. You have to face 'The Baddie'. If you go into this stage with all of your lives intact, you are going to be confident and sooooo ready to take this on! But if you go into this with just one life, your confidence will be low, you will not believe in yourself. Now If this baddie manages to overcome you, what happens?

Its ok, you will just have to go back to the start of the level again.

Off you go back at the beginning, but this time you know exactly what you have to do! You are filled with confidence. You avoid all of the things that are there trying to slip you up. You can complete it faster because you are prepared for all of the things trying to catch you out! Now when you approach the end, you pause the game for a moment, take a breath and then you go for it! You have completed the level! Success!

Onto the next level....

So how does this relate to your life?

When you start playing the game, you have everyone around you supporting you and cheering you on. It is like learning to walk. Each time you fall, someone cheers you on. They say 'Come on! You can do it!' You get back up and keep on trying, time and time again until you get it. Not once did someone say 'Stop trying'. Because they knew the potential to walk was inside of you! If they thought you could not do it, they would get you the support you needed!

The first few Game-of-Life levels go like this. Easy learning, and fun! But each level holds new lessons. In level 1 you get to unlock learning to navigate friendships and knowledge. Then you have to spend 6 hours a day learning at a thing called school!

For some, this level can be quite easy to get through. But for others, not so easy! Never compare yourself to others, they are not playing your game and you are not playing theirs! On this level, you learn new skills and boundaries. You get to make new friends and learn how to communicate.

You begin to learn about who you are in this game of life. And how to deal with the emotional things that life brings; the hurt, the upsets, the love, the joy, and the laughter! Know that all of these feelings and emotions are welcome.

This level has more challenges than the earlier levels, but you learn and grow from each situation. The better choices you make, the easier it is for you to find your way. You have to work through many similar levels over the years. Each level bringing its own lessons and challenges.

As you complete each level, there is always another one! This never stops. But every level is an opportunity to better yourself. *You* get to choose how you show up in it. *You* get to decide how you want to play the game!

Take a moment and think about how you can relate this to your life.

Write down all of the things that you have managed to overcome in your life that have allowed you to break through to a new level.

Life is just a game, it is our mission to learn how we can navigate it.

First of all, what kind of player do you want to be?

Do you want to be the one that shows up and keeps finding a way around every difficult stage? Someone with an 'I can do this' attitude?

Or do you want to be the type of player that gives up at the first banana skin?

What I know for certain is that if you want to succeed at this game of life you have to be willing to keep on going; keep on dealing with whatever comes your way, with the deepest level of self-responsibility.

Write down what kind of player you want to be in this game? Confident, fun, powerful, a leader, kind, compassionate, healthy, loving! You get to choose how you show up in life.

Once you have chosen who you want to be, it is time to make a commitment to yourself. This is a great lesson to learn. You have to start to show up as that person in your life. You do this by keeping your word to yourself, so if you say you are going to do something, you follow through. This builds trust and confidence with yourself. You watch the language you use, how you talk to yourself and others.

Dealing with difficult levels and losing.

Not every level is going to be easy. You are going to find some of them very tough. Life will throw lots of 'lessons' (banana skins) your way. Until you start to understand them, they will keep on showing up.

Can you think of any situations/events that keep showing up in your life? Write them down and look for patterns. Maybe there are lessons you have to learn that you have missed.

Losing a level. Is it truly a failure?

I want to tell you a secret…You know you cannot fail! Read that again.

It is a huge lesson. Very powerful. You may 'feel' like you have failed; you may even be told you have failed. But you *know* that you cannot fail at anything – you can only have learning experiences.

When you are playing the game and it does not go to plan, you fail a level. It is these failures that make you who you are. They help you grow. They teach you, stretch you. If you go into every situation knowing that it may not turn out how you want it to, you may not complete and win the level the first time…but each time things do not go to plan you will learn something. You do not give up; you pick yourself up and try and try again, until you get the outcome you desire.

Desires.

You have the power to create whatever you desire. If you show up every day of your life as the character that you choose. If you take the actions, keep authentic, behave with kindness and compassion; all this behaves like a magnet. Your life begins to gravitate in the direction you choose.

You just have to DECIDE! When you face everything in life head-on, not in a forceful way, but with certainty; When you believe so DEEPLY in yourself you know that NOTHING can stop you. Believing this, reminding yourself every day that regardless of what happens you know where you are going and there is only one outcome and that is to WIN!

But what happens if you get stuck on a level? The solution is simple. ALWAYS ask for help! Ask for help from someone who has completed it before you. It does not have to be someone you know. Or maybe you find the answers in a book; or on YouTube.

I am not going to sugarcoat things. Life will not always be easy. We are all here living a human experience. The experience allows us to feel the highs and the lows. If you feel overwhelmed and feel like giving up - reach out for help, choose a safe person to share everything you are feeling!

Write down who your safe person is.

When you need support reach out to them. Let them know that you have chosen them as your number one support when things are tough. They will be honored and will take their responsibility seriously.

Hold the standard of who you are.

Girls I would love you to look at your life as a game, a game that you are always going to show up for because you are in this game to WIN! Step into your Personal Power and decide who you are showing up as in this lifetime. When you get knocked down, brush yourself down and move forward....no matter what! You have the future in the palm of your hands. Never let anyone tell you that you cannot do anything. You have to be the one to take personal responsibility, standing tall to say, "watch me" CLAIM IT! Create the energy around you not of arrogance but that of knowing! A deep belief in yourself from certainty and love.

Then celebrate each day, celebrate life, celebrate all that you are and all that you are becoming. Spend each day in gratitude. Feel EVERY day, even the hard days, because those are the days that stretch you and allow you to grow!

Do not get caught up in negativity and bitchiness. Be a leader, not a follower. When you see this happening, do not get involved. CHOOSE to take the higher road. You will feel so much better lifting people up, rather than pulling them down.

I want to leave you with this:

I BELIEVE IN YOU
YOU ARE WORTHY
YOU ARE LOVE
YOU ARE UNSTOPPABLE

You have the potential to be, do and have ANYTHING you want in this life! Never allow anyone to tell you otherwise! Go out and change the world! We need more young woman just like you to stand in their brilliance. Be the example to all of your friends, bring them along with you. Lead by example! BELIEVE IN YOURSELF.

Sending so much love to you!

Make positive choices, go out and be the change in this world.

You've got this

xx

CHAPTER THREE

Handling Heartbreak

Having your heart broken is something we will all experience in our lives. A rite of passage.

Sounds depressing right? But look at it another way: if you have not had your heartbroken, you have probably not really lived your life. And who does not want a life well-lived?

Heartbreak comes in many forms. Losing a family member, or a beloved family pet; the end of a friendship; the divorce of your parents; or from the break-up of a romantic relationship. Heartbreak is heartbreak, no matter what causes it.

Why we experience it might be different, but *what* we experience is remarkably similar.

This is a good starting point. When heartbreak happens, it can feel as though you are the only person in the world going through it. But lots of people have felt the same as you, and many more will. We can all benefit from understanding that. And it can help us learn to feel better more quickly.

In this chapter, I am going to focus on romantic heartbreak because there are things I have learned about it in my life that I wish I had known as a teenager.

I was 18 the first time my heart got broken.

My relationship with my first serious boyfriend ended and I thought my world had ended with it. Because that is what happens when you experience true heartbreak. You cannot believe that you will ever feel ok again.

I say 'true' heartbreak. Why? It is easy to throw the word 'heartbroken' around. You are heartbroken when your parents refuse to buy you the latest trainers. You are heartbroken when the person you like has not asked you to be their prom date. These situations are 'upsetting'; they are not 'true' heartbreak.

When your heart is truly broken, the pain is intense. It is unmistakable. Like nothing else you have ever been through. It feels as though your body and mind are screaming. You may feel as though you are going crazy. You cannot find the words to explain how torn apart you feel. You do not feel able to connect to anything or anybody. All you can hear is 'white noise', like static on a radio. Like walking through fog. The hurt is so bad, so deep, and so all-consuming that you cannot believe that anyone has gone through it and come out the other side. You find it impossible to talk about and make others understand because words are not enough.

You feel as though you will never find peace. Never find solid ground to stand on.

But you will.

I am living proof. My heart has been broken many times. I could tell you many stories, but perhaps another time, or another place. What really matters is that I survived to tell the tale!

I found ways to love again and learned that it was ok to feel vulnerable. I am proud of how I managed to survive and move on. It is not that my heartbreaks were not horrible - they were devastating - but over time I have learned to understand them; figure out what is happening and discover what it takes to heal. And how I can have control over that, at a time when everything feels out of control.

I was a long way from that place of understanding when I was 18.

I really had no idea of what heartbreak was.

My parents had been married 'forever'. My sister had not experienced it yet. Nor had any of my closest friends.

There was no life raft to cling to. Noone to help me make sense of what was happening - emotionally and physically. That was part of what I needed to learn: that heartbreak is not just an emotional experience. There are physical effects too.

So right now, as you are reading this. Here I am. Your heartbreak life raft.

If you have been through heartbreak in the past or are going through it right now (if you are, I am so sorry) or if it is yet to find you, I want you to know you are not alone. I want you to understand that you do not need to 'suffer' it; there are strategies you can adopt that will make it easier. They will not stop you from going through it, but they will help ease the process.

I am a fan of knowledge. I believe that by understanding the basic facts of what is happening to us emotionally and physically, we can learn to cope better. Discovering some tools you can use to get you through, will help you throughout your life. Finding ways to figure out the root cause of why you are feeling the way you feel can help you change the stories you tell yourself and how you respond to them. Creating a more positive and mature mindset that you can depend on and use whenever you need it.

I am not a doctor. Not a medic or a psychologist. I am just a woman who has experienced and researched the kinds of heartbreak you are or will be, going through. When it comes to explaining the basics of what happens when our hearts 'break', I have no complicated science to base my answers on, just some simple principles.

Making sense of it

My favourite word is 'discombobulated.'

It means that you are so confused that you do not know which way is up and you probably cannot even spell your own name!

Heartbreak is discombobulating. It throws you so off-balance that your mind and body are spinning.

I learned about the physiology, physics and chemistry of heartbreak from an incredible man called Guy Winch. What I learned left me stunned, but relieved. Suddenly it all made sense. The 'my heart is actually breaking' feeling that I had experienced. When I discovered that our bodies and brains have a physical reaction to heartbreak as well as an emotional one, I started to feel better. It did not change how much my heartbreak and my memories of it hurt, but I started to feel less 'crazy' about what I had gone through. It made something that had felt so abnormal, feel normal.

Feeling like you are going mad during heartbreak adds to the mental burden, so it is important to learn that you are not. What you are feeling is the body's natural response. You are not really losing your mind!

Here is why.

- *Your emotions*

Heartbreak is a form of grief. Something we go through after any loss. No one can say how long grieving will take. With heartbreak, in particular, you will feel like you are making progress one minute and then slide down the slippery slope into hopelessness again the next. Research shows that when we experience it, especially romantic heartbreak, the parts of our brain that are activated are the areas connected with addiction. Scary, right? To think that heartbreak creates the kind of cravings we would associate with taking drugs is, quite literally, mind-blowing.

But knowing this can help us. All the things we feel when we go through heartbreak

- feeling agitated and restless, our inability to focus on anything else - all begins to make sense. The need to get the next 'hit' of that person, to achieve the 'high' we feel when we are with them… becomes overwhelming. The thing is it is natural to feel all of it. There are chemical and physical reasons for what is going on. It is what the broken-hearted go through. You are not alone.

- *Your body*

We all underestimate the physical impact of a 'broken' heart on our body.

Scientists have shown that the pain your body feels during romantic heartbreak is equal to significant physical pain - think 8 out of 10 pain where 10 was defined as 'unbearable'!

If you were experiencing that amount of physical pain, you would not force yourself to keep functioning at school, college or in daily life. You would give yourself a break, take some over-the-counter medicine and let yourself rest.

As Guy Winch puts it so eloquently: *You would not tell someone with a broken leg to just 'walk it off'. But we take that approach to ourselves (and others) when it comes to emotional pain.*

During heartbreak, you need to understand that you may experience as much physical pain from this 'emotional' event, as you would if you had undergone physical trauma. Be as kind to yourself in your recovery.

Making it worse

- *Hiding*

When your heart breaks and your mind and body are in 'crisis', it is natural to feel exhausted. Just breathing in and out becomes an enormous effort. Something that you really have to think about. It is not surprising that you struggle to get out of bed and face the world.

The tough truth is that hiding away is the worst thing you can do. You will feel lonelier and more isolated.

- *Stalking*

Social media is a nightmare for this. Yet whether you are looking endlessly through your ex's social media posts or physically following them around (let's be honest, we have all done it!), the surge of excitement you feel is a temporary fix. You feel so good! But that feeling is quickly followed by the addict's 'crash'; you will end up feeling worse, not better.

- *Blaming*

Beating yourself up for everything that went wrong in your past relationship will not help you move forward. Regret is a wasted, energy-sapping emotion. You cannot change the past. You need action and reaction to break a relationship, so accept that there were faults on both sides. Punishing yourself will not help in any way.

- *Explaining*

Sometimes a relationship just is not meant to be. You can never know what is going on for someone else. Their stuff – their feelings, thoughts, history, and decisions – that is *their* thing. You cannot ever understand all of it. Chances are, they don't understand it either. Trying to 'make sense of it all' to understand 'why' is fruitless; it will drive you nuts!

Making it better

- *Caring*

When your heart breaks you often stop taking care of yourself. The stress created in your body affects your immune system, meaning you can get sick more easily. Sleep suffers, eating suffers, health suffers. You may lack the energy to look after yourself or feel that you do not deserve to feel well. The opposite is true. This is a time for extreme self-love.

Get lots of rest. Eat healthy foods. Speak kindly to yourself. All these things will speed up your recovery.

- *Focusing*

With our emotions out of balance, our view of the world becomes confused too. Wanting desperately to see your ex and trying to understand what went wrong, means that you will spend a lot of time thinking about everything that was good about them and the relationship. Focus on looking at them in a balanced way. Write a list of the pros and cons of them/the relationship. Get friends to help you if necessary. It is not about slagging them off. Just because they were not right for you does not make them a bad person.

- *Re-connecting*

Being part of a couple changes us. 'I' becomes 'We'. Losing that connection can leave us feeling lost. A good way to bounce back after heartbreak is to reconnect with who you are. What are the things you can spend more time on now that you do not have to consider that person? Are there hobbies and people that you can give your attention to again? What have you learnt from this experience that you can take forward? Get excited about re-discovering you.

- *Progressing*

During heartbreak, it is easy to feel 'stuck'. One of the most positive ways to get over your heartache is to feel like you are making progress with something. Anything. Pick a task, a project or set a goal and take those first steps towards it. You will immediately feel like the world is turning for you again and that you will not feel this sad forever. I promise that you will not!

Making habits for life

I cannot stop you suffering heartbreak. In fact, I hope I don't! Because loving people is one of the greatest joys of being human - we just need to pick the right ones to love. I hope that I have helped you to understand what happens and given you some ideas on how best to cope with it.

Here are some general practices that will equip you for life:

- *Standards*
  - o Set standards for yourself.
  - o What behaviour are you willing and unwilling to tolerate from others?
  - o Be clear about what they are and do not compromise – even when you come under pressure to do so (and you will).
  - o Stand firm.

- *Vulnerability*
  - o It is ok to be vulnerable. I would encourage it.
  - o See vulnerability as a strength.
  - o You will see who your tribe are and who they are not based on how they respond to you sharing your most vulnerable self.
  - o Choose the ones who choose to walk alongside you.

- *Confidence*
  - o Know that no one 'gives' you confidence. So, no one can take it away.
  - o Understand that your confidence comes from within you, so you control it.
  - o Know who you are, set boundaries for what you will accept and keeping that promise to yourself.

Finally. Do not let a fear of heartbreak stop you from loving. You got this!

CHAPTER FOUR

Relationship to Self

Beautiful girl, I love you! All of you. Yes, you. You do not need to change a thing.

I love you just the way you are.

Do you wish that someone would say these words to you? Do you wish someone would love you just for you? Do you wish there was someone in your life, who does not want to change you? Someone who thinks you are perfect, just as you are?

I did, especially when I was a teenager. So much confusion and frustration with my parents and friends. And feeling very uncomfortable with all the changes my body was going through.

As I got older, I learned that I had to be the one to say these words to myself before anybody else could say them to me. It took me years, and it was not until I was well into my forties (with some help from a few friends and some inspirational mentors) that I began to develop a loving and healthy relationship with myself.

You may be asking yourself what does *"having a relationship yourself"* mean?

In this chapter, we are going to explore what it means to have a relationship with yourself and I am going to give you some tools to use to help *you* build a healthy relationship with yourself.

You already have relationships. With your mother, father, brother, sister, teachers, and friends. But the most important relationship is the one you have with yourself, and here is why it is so important. The relationship you have with yourself will set the tone for every relationship you have in your life.

When I was younger, I found the concept of self-love embarrassing and uncomfortable. Because I did not understand it, and I was never taught how or what it meant to love myself.

Take a moment to ask yourself this:

"What sort of relationship do I have with the people in my life?"

When you think about being in a relationship with someone, what do you expect from them? Do you expect them to make you feel loved? Safe? Happy?

Do you expect your teachers to be kind? Do you expect your parents to be there for you when you need them? Do you expect your friends to be there to make you laugh? Do you expect the people in your life to speak to you respectfully and communicate their feelings?

I bet you answered yes to at least one of these questions. Having a relationship with yourself involves many of the same things.

I would like you to reflect on whether you set these same expectations for yourself.

You cannot expect others to give you what you cannot give to yourself. If you do not value yourself, then why should you expect other people to do so? We do not look after or protect what we do not hold in high regard

I once heard a teacher say something that has stuck with me for years. He said: *"The most important words you will utter are the ones that you say to yourself, about yourself, when you are by yourself."*

So, how do *you* speak to yourself? What kind of words do you use? Do you use kind and gentle words? Or judgemental and shameful words?

We all have an inner voice that guides our decision-making. Is your inside voice helpful or harmful?

If you say mean things to yourself, you are not alone. But, together, we are going to learn to replace your inner dialogue with kinder, gentler, more compassionate words. This may not be easy, but the more you work at it, the easier it will become. You will start having a healthy relationship with yourself.

You have probably been taught to be kind and considerate to others, but have you been taught to be kind and considerate to yourself?

The questions below will help you create a more positive conversation with yourself.

How do you want others to love you? Here are some examples:

- I want to be loved unconditionally.
- I want others to care about things that matter to me.
- I want others to speak to me with kind, respectful words, and demonstrate acts of kindness.
- I want others to treat me with respect.
- I want to be hugged and told 'I love you'.

Write your answer below:

_____

_____

_____

_____

_____

The relationship you have with yourself will play a huge role in determining who your friends are, who you date, and even the jobs that you choose. If you want others to treat you with kindness and respect, you need to start treating *yourself* with kindness and respect.

Start by forgiving yourself for not knowing sooner how to have a loving relationship with yourself. Forgiveness is an act of self-love and self-compassion.

We can only do better when we know better.

Here are eight steps to help you achieve a healthier, happier, and more positive relationship with yourself.

1. RECOGNIZING AND CHANGING NEGATIVE SELF TALK

We all have an inner voice that is constantly talking to us, telling us what we are doing and how we are feeling. Sometimes that voice can be self-critical and judgmental. That inner voice plays a major role in our decision-making.

The first step is to recognize when you are engaging in negative self-talk. Telling yourself, "I am not loveable", or "I am not smart enough", is harmful to your self-esteem, confidence, and your overall health. Try replacing negative self-talk with positive.

For example:

Instead of saying: "I am not lovable" say "I am a loving person and I'm working on loving myself."

Or instead of saying: "I am not smart enough" try "I'm trying my best at school and when I don't understand an assignment, I will ask a supportive person for help."

Can you feel how different each of these statements feels in your body?

When you speak to yourself as you would a good friend, with encouraging and supportive vocabulary, you begin to feel better about yourself. Even like yourself more!

Practice this exercise daily. The more you do it, the easier it will become and the better your relationship with yourself will be. The more you will like yourself. Be kind to yourself.

2. LISTEN TO YOUR HEART

When you are faced with a difficult decision, feeling confused about something, or having a hard time sorting out your emotions, I want you to try this exercise.

Find a quiet place where you can have some privacy (even if that is in the bathroom). Sit in a comfortable position and place your right hand on your heart. Begin by slowing down your breathing. Then ask yourself these four powerful questions:

1. *"What do I need right now?"*
2. *"What do I need to know about this situation right now?"*
3. *"What is the best decision for me right now?"*
4. *"What are my emotions trying to tell me?"*

We all have a wise little voice that whispers to us. Those whispers are your heart trying to communicate with you. That is your divine self. Take a few moments to pause, breathe, and listen.

3. MAKE A LIST OF YOUR ACCOMPLISHMENTS

I think we all need to be reminded of how awesome we are!

Create a list of everything you have accomplished, big or small. Anything: from making the soccer team to riding a bike. Or getting your yellow belt in karate.

It does not matter what the accomplishment is, this list is to remind you of how much you have achieved and how capable and worthy you are.

Reviewing this list will help you feel proud of yourself, and that will help you feel better about yourself. Creating a stronger relationship with yourself.

4. GET TO KNOW YOURSELF

What kind of movies do you like?
Do like to draw?
Do you play sports?
What kind of books do you like to read?
If you could travel anywhere in the world, where would you go?

Answering questions like these is a great way to get to know yourself better. As you get older, your likes, views, and preferences naturally change. Getting to know what you like, and dislike is fun and interesting.

Answer the questions below:

* I am interested in

_____

* I worry about

_____

* I am really good at

_____

* _____ makes me feel sad.

★ _____ makes me laugh.

★ _____ makes me feel happy.

*I would like to get better at

_____

*I have difficulty with

_____

*I love _____ about myself.

You can add your own questions too. Trying new things is a great way to discover something new about yourself. You may be surprised how much you like or dislike something. Go ahead: give yourself permission to try something new!

5. COMPARING OURSELVES TO OTHERS

We all compare ourselves to others. But why waste time focussing on other people's lives instead of your own? When you compare other's strengths to your weaknesses, it hurts. It can lead to feelings of self-doubt and inferiority and can lower your confidence.

Comparing yourself is also unfair. We are all different, living in different families with different cultures and experiences.

Albert Einstein wrote, *"Everybody is a genius. But if you judge a fish by its ability to climb a tree, it will live its whole life believing that it is stupid."*

You are a unique young woman, unlike anybody else in the entire world. Focus on your strengths and what you do well. The world needs your unique self.

6. BOUNDARIES

What are boundaries, and why are they so important anyway?

Boundaries are basic guidelines that tell others how you want to be treated and what levels of behaviour you will accept from other people.

Boundaries are an essential part of a healthy relationship with others, and they are important in your relationship with yourself.

Let me give you some examples.

- I am okay with following each other on social media but I'm not okay with sharing our passwords.
- I am cool with texting each other, but not after 10:00 pm.
- I am okay with holding hands in public, but I am not okay with kissing in public.

You teach others how to treat you. This is a very important point. You get what you tolerate. So, if your best friend makes fun of how you dress and it bothers you, but you don't say anything, he or she will keep doing it.

Setting a boundary is telling your friend that those comments hurt your feelings, and if they continue to make them, you can no longer spend time together.

It can feel uncomfortable setting boundaries, especially if you worry about what other people will think. But you will find that people who care about you will listen, respect your feelings, and make changes so that their behavior does not upset you.

7. SPEND TIME ALONE

Think about when you spend time alone with a good friend or a family member. This is when you get to know each other better and grow closer. The same applies when you create space to spend alone time with yourself.

Spend your alone time doing anything you like. Working on a puzzle, listening to your favorite music, drawing or painting, going for a walk in nature, or even meditating. What you decide to do with your alone time will be unique to you, and that is okay. What is important is that you make time for yourself daily, even if just for a few minutes.

Once you begin to practice this habit you will find that you will look forward to your alone time, and it will deepen your relationship with yourself.

8. JOURNALING

If you have never journaled before, do not worry. There is no right or wrong way to do it. Journaling is a way to get your emotions onto paper and to express yourself. Especially if you have a hard time communicating what you are feeling.

It can help you figure out your feelings. Writing helps to slow down your thinking and allows you to connect to a deeper part of yourself.

Think about it as writing a letter to your best friend

Beautiful girl, I love you! All of you. Yes, you. There is no need to change a thing.

I love you just the way you are.

CHAPTER FIVE

Even when your past feels like it weighs you down, it is the very thing carrying you towards your purpose.

This is the part I always find difficult, describing myself. I think it is because I am not who I used to be. I am still on a journey of discovering who I am, so how could I possibly tell you about me?

Let me start with the basics. I am 25, from Hertfordshire but living in London, I am a youth worker. I have huge ambitions for my future, and future generations and I have a very big heart.

But…I procrastinate. I get comfortable, I cry, I fail and 70% of the time I convince myself I am dying or losing the plot. So yeah, that is me in a round-about way. Or at least parts of who I am. I am here to tell my story, not only to inform and inspire you but to help myself come to terms with things too.

To put it bluntly, I was a reckless teenager with substance misuse issues. At the time I had no idea they were 'issues'. I hid things well from my parents. I lived to party and have fun. My life motto was "I can sleep when I'm dead". That attitude lead to many sleepless nights. Out raving and chatting rubbish until God knows what time the next morning. Or even the morning after that on many occasions.

I was dabbling in cocaine, mephedrone, MDMA, pills, weed and a mega load of alcohol.

Growing up I lived in a small area, and there were no youth centres or easily accessible things to do. We had to create our own fun. And that is what we did. I am not going to go through 5 years-worth of teenage memories because although that would be a good read, about 60% of it is totally inappropriate!

Admittedly the times we had were hilarious and definitely life-changing. I would not change that for the world. But eventually, the fun started to go a bit wrong. I noticed a problem in some of the people around me and the number of drugs they were doing. After losing a close friend when I was 17, life started to feel very real, and I became a little bit more cautious. However, I am a raver at heart. Having access to an ID that got me into places meant that I carried on. I did not want to let my lifestyle go.

Between the ages of 17-19, I pretty much raved every weekend, with a few house sessions in between. I love festivals too. One summer I attended 12! Oh, how I wish I could do that now!

My physical and mental health held up pretty well considering how badly I was abusing my body. I decided I wanted to get out of my local area, and my comfort zone to go live it up somewhere else in the world. In May 2015 I went to the Greek island of Zante with 2 friends. The plan was to stay for the season. lasted all of 6 weeks!

While I was there I had an epiphany. I realised that I wanted to do something more with my life. So, when I got back I decided to apply for university. A rogue decision for someone that had dropped out of college twice and never enjoyed education.

Despite my previous experience and with the help of my incredible father, I wrote an outstanding letter detailing what inspired me to study psychology and I received an unconditional offer! It was July 2015.

Knowing that I was off to Uni in September I decided to make the most of my summer. And I did. Until the night that changed my life.

A simple night out that went terribly wrong. The reason I am sharing all this information with you.

I was at a festival on the Friday but stayed sober and drove because I knew I was going out the next night too. I was sensible enough never to do illicit drugs when driving. But I was taking pro plus caffeine tablets, drinking red bull, and doing a few balloons here and there.

By the way, I was on antibiotics at the time and not supposed to drink alcohol. But smart little me thought it would still be ok to do MDMA on the Saturday. I honestly did not even do half as much as I usually would. But when I got back to my friend's home I could not sleep and thought smoking a zoot would 'level me out'. It had the total opposite effect.

My heart started beating so fast that I had to wake everyone up and call 111. They said we had an hour to get to the A&E. I do not think I have ever been in a faster car in my life! My heart was pounding and my chest tightening. My head was filled with mad thoughts going through my head about whether I was about to die or not.

I was in the hospital for 7 hours on a heart monitor. I remember vividly that my resting heart rate was around 123 beats per minute. I was hyperventilating.

There was a time when a group of nurses were surrounding me speaking about whether they would need to use the defibrillator - serious stuff!!! Everything else was a bit of a blur, as you can probably imagine.

This was a pivotal moment for me. The fun, calm and outgoing Meg I had always been got a massive wake-up call. Both my body and mind went into overdrive.

I developed mental health issues that I now know to be PTSD and panic disorder. For weeks I could not be left alone without having a panic attack. At the time I did not know that this was what they were. I constantly felt like I was going to have a heart attack and be rushed back to the hospital! I could barely go out in public. I was an anxious wreck on the sofa.

My experience made me so much more scared to go to Uni. But somehow, I managed to deal with my anxiety and I went. I am so glad I did. Overall, it was an amazing experience. Something I am so proud to have achieved. My mental health was pretty stable during those years. I had fallen back in love with life.

But after I graduated, things seriously declined. The past 3 years have been the hardest of my life.

When you are in your 20's and you finish Uni you lose that routine. There is so much pressure to have everything worked out. This did not help me at all. I felt lost and confused; like I was falling apart. I had no career direction in mind and very little money to keep me afloat.

Moving back home was never an option for me. I had come so far, I did not want to feel like I was taking backwards steps in life. To be brutally honest, I considered suicide on many occasions. Not because I was sad but because I was so fed up that I could not control my mental and physical anxiety! I had so many panic attacks that I almost became agoraphobic. I literally had to force myself to do anything.

For about 2 years I was in a state of de-personalisation. I felt as though I was not in my own body; as if I could blackout at any time. The thoughts seemed irrational because depersonalisation comes with brain fog and confusion. But it felt so real at the time. I even took myself to A&E and said there is something wrong with me. The only way I could describe it was that I felt like I was not real. I had to do a lot of work on myself to identify and overcome this. I will touch on some of the techniques I used a bit further on.

I really lost myself during these years. I was scared to die but also scared to live. I had no idea what to do.

This is where my journey to self-love and realisation started, and why I am here sharing this. I have researched, tried, and tested so much of life that I never knew existed. I have never accepted medication for my mental illness as I am so determined to find ways to naturally better myself. But I do not judge anyone who chooses to take medication. What works for one of us will not work for all of us!

Healing is a linear journey. There may be many setbacks and it is easy to feel disheartened. But the main thing I promised myself was to never give up. Being anxious 90% of the time brings a different perspective to your life. You have to re-learn how to stay calm and manage your emotions. Difficult at the best of times!

I always laughed when people told me to meditate. I could not sit still for 5 minutes under instruction, let alone by choice! BUT I tried it anyway. I failed many times until I found what worked for me and now? I LOVE IT! Meditating does bring peace of mind even if for only a short period. Think of it in the same way as exercise for the body - short breaks are necessary for growth. It is the same with thoughts. Giving your mind a moment to pause helps SO much.

I have done a lot of research into diet, the mind and the physical sensations experienced with mental illness. I wanted to identify anything I was putting into my body that may have been contributing to the problem. In 2019 I spent the whole year completely sober, not even a sip of alcohol. This helped me with discipline and determination but also allowed me to meet myself again and know who I was without the influence of any substances. I was the most sober I had been since I was 15!

I lost friendships throughout this time because some people could not understand why I had to do it. Although this was upsetting it was also eye-opening. It further cemented my belief that you should do what is best for you. No matter what other people think!

There are various health foods and supplements that have supported my healing. I could probably write an entire book just about this! Some excellent calming herbs that work for me are Ashwagandha and Maca root.

Something which has saved me from insomnia and night-time panic attacks is CBD oil. It has helped me fall in love with sleep again! I no longer think 'I will sleep when I am dead'. My thought process is now more like 'Where is my bed?!' Oh, how times have changed.

Self-growth and reflection are amazing. It is something I never knew would be part of my world, but I am grateful it is. In my career, I think back to my teenage self and the positive influence I needed, and I apply this when I am working with young people. I believe that better education on drugs and their long-term effects on the brain and mental health is essential for helping younger generations to make wiser decisions.

Please do not be a reckless Meg. Although I got here in the end, it could have been a much easier path!

There is much more to my story, and I would love to share it with the world, but I cannot fit it all into one chapter. Watch this space for more to come.

If you take anything from reading this today let it be this: even when your past feels like it weighs you down, it is the very thing carrying you towards your purpose- GO WITH IT!!!

Oh yeah and don't worry about what other people think!!!

One love, Meg xxx

CHAPTER SIX

You are not alone

Once again, I found myself sitting on my bedroom floor in a pile of clothes. My head in my hands, and tears pouring down my face. Anger and hopelessness consuming my body.

Why do I have to feel this way?
Why does life have to be so hard?
I am so frustrated.
I am lost.
No one understands me.
I am alone.

I stand up, still crying. I start looking for clothes that will look right. My heart is pounding, my stomach is upset. I just want a day where I do not have to impress anyone. It is 8:00 am and I have 30 minutes to get ready. There is no way I can do my hair and makeup and find clothes in that time.

The chatter in my head consumes me. I want it to shut up, but it just goes on and on.

I cannot go to school looking this way.
I hate high school, it is hell.
Everyone is so mean to each other.
I just want to stay home.

But I know my mom will be waiting for me and I do not want to disappoint her. The tears flow and I want to scream at the top of my lungs. More thoughts fill my head.

You are not good enough.
You cannot do it; you are going to disappoint people.
I hate myself.

This was a typical day for me.

When I started in 9th grade my world changed. I began seeing things differently. Earlier in childhood, I had had difficult moments; being made fun of and bullied. But 9th grade brought this to a whole new level.

My friends turned their backs on me. There was exclusion and racism. People got into physical fights, stole, cheated, and lied. I could feel a collective sadness amongst the teens. I did not understand how things could change so quickly. My world was ripped out from underneath me.

Two months after starting high school I was hospitalised. I had been isolating myself in my room, not wanting to talk or eat. My mom and dad had no idea how to help me. I thought I had no choice so let them take me to hospital.

For the first day or two, I did not talk to the doctors. It was awful. I was locked on a ward with people who were very ill. Way out of my comfort zone and scared. I knew I had to start talking if I wanted to go home. The doctors asked stupid, pointless. They were never going to get to the root cause of how I was feeling. So, I told them what they wanted to hear so that I could go home.

I carried on doing my best to survive adolescence. I suppressed most of what I was feeling. It was just too painful. On the outside, I looked like I was happy and successful. But inside I was lost. I was just doing what I needed to do to get through life, going through the motions to survive.

I had been raised with good morals and clear values, so I knew what I was supposed to do to have a successful life, or what other people thought a successful life was. I went on and achieved those things, but I was never really happy.

In my mid-20s I started working with a group called Youth Net. We went into high schools to talk to groups of teens about mental health, illness, and suicide. We discussed life. We asked them about their challenges. What always came up was that they felt isolated and alone.

Like no one understood them. That they had to please people. They had to look and be a certain way to be accepted. They were always shocked to know that their peers felt the same way.

I listened and wished that I had had a platform to talk openly about what I was experiencing. Not with doctors who wanted to figure out what was wrong with me. But with other teenagers that could relate to me. I would have realised that what I was experiencing was normal and that I was not alone.

I am sharing some of my story now so that you know you are not alone either.

Your Brain in Puberty

The teenage brain is quite complex. I am not going to get into all the science. If you are interested, you can just Google it. But I will share a couple of interesting bits!

Your brain is still maturing, and it will continue to develop into your 20's.

The prefrontal cortex is an area of your brain used for decision-making, planning and self-control. It is the last part of your brain to mature. You do have frontal lobe capabilities but the signals you receive are not getting to the back of your brain fast enough to regulate emotions.

This is why you may have more risk-taking and impulsive behaviors. You may be forgetful and find that you are not always able to think ahead or problem-solve. And if that is not enough, there are major changes taking place in your limbic system at the same time!

This system is reward-seeking, which means it is always looking for things to make you feel good. Because the limbic system develops earlier and faster than the prefrontal cortex, the desire for rewards and social pressures overrides rational thinking. Until it catches up!

This explains why I was having a hard time choosing clothes and was concerned about looking a certain way to attend school. My thoughts about the situation were distorted and I simply could not see that.

I was not able to think rationally about what I was experiencing.

Phew, I wish I had known that my brain was just under construction!

Identity Shifting

OK, this is a huge one. As we move into adolescence, we are constantly changing and maturing. We can be very confused about what we want in life and who we are.

You continue to grow physically, cognitively, and emotionally. Changing from a child into an adult. You will start to develop more advanced patterns of reasoning, a stronger sense of self and start seeking to find your own identity.

It is a stressful time. It involves new emotions, and you feel the need to develop new types of relationships. On top of all that you will feel an increased sense of responsibility and independence.

Even in my 40's, I am still trying to figure this out!

Looking back, knowing what I know now, I can see I had very few role models. Those that I had were amazing and I aspired to be like them. But when I wasn't, I felt like a failure. I did not know that I had other options.

I found myself continually trying to live up to what I believed was expected of me by society. Always trying to make other people happy. It was exhausting. My life was consumed with activities, ideas and behaviours that were not my own.

I even chose a job that I thought was ideal. Because it was secure and provided the income that I believed was important. This left me more unhappy, lost and alone.

Now I know that I do not have to be like anybody else. I get to decide who I am. You get to decide who *you* are! You do not have to settle for a career that does not bring you joy. You do not have to participate in activities out of obligation, and you absolutely do not have to act and look a certain way to be accepted.

Explore! Find activities, people and things that make you feel good. Read books, watch videos. Discover new ideas, beliefs and tools that make sense to *you*, not anyone else. Know that you do not have to have it all figured out now.

This is one of the greatest blessings in life. You get to choose what path you take and the speed you travel at. You get to take as many detours as you want and enjoy taking them.

Remember, it is OK to be different. In fact, it is important! Because then you are being yourself. Trust me, that is when you will be the most fulfilled.

Energy Shifting

This is one of my favourite things! Did you know, that if we look at our hands under a super high-powered microscope that we are not actually solid?

We are all made up of energy, the same energy that makes up EVERYTHING in this universe. How cool is that?

Energy vibrates at all different frequencies. We create vibrations in our body through our feelings and emotions. Feelings and emotions are created through our thoughts.

Are you still following me?

So, if we have happy, positive, and encouraging thoughts it will create a frequency in the body that aligns with those thoughts.

This may be more challenging in our teens. Our minds are developing, and our thoughts are all over the place. I believe that if you are aware that your thoughts are not always clear and if you can learn to observe them, then you have an opportunity to shift them.

I know that this can seem overwhelming, especially when you are overcome with huge negative emotions. If you find yourself stuck in this space, there are some things I recommend that can help shift the thoughts and energy.

- Get outside and get some air
- Find five things you can see, hear, feel, smell and touch
- Journal
- Scream in a pillow
- Punch a pillow
- Jump, shake, run – move your body
- Breath

Some of these may sound silly but give them a try. You never know, they may work.

Once you find a way to shift the negative energy, try to focus on the things you are grateful for. No matter how big or small. It could be a pet, a friend, food and water, your favorite pillow or blanket.

Even after years of practice this can be challenging, but I know you can do it! With practice you will see how it can help.

While we are exploring the connection between thought and energy, there is another topic I invite you to explore in more depth. The conscious and subconscious mind. Learning how our brains work and about the power of thought is important and fascinating.

Well, we have reached the end of my chapter. There is so much more that I would love to show you.

I have shared a few of the things that I wish I had known. Things that would have helped me to navigate my teenage years and the rest of my life. I continue to learn and grow every single day.

Remember that there will always be challenges in life. I invite you to see them as blessings. Because they are teaching us lessons that do not always make sense in the moment.

But one day you will see how they have led you to this exact perfect point.

Remember that when a challenge arises to it is only in that moment, and the moment will pass, it is not forever.

Always be kind and loving to yourself. Treat yourself like you would treat your best friend. Keep learning, exploring, and searching for things that you love.

I want to thank you from the bottom of my heart for reading my story. I am sending love to every single one of you. Holding you in my heart.

Know that you are great, worthy, and perfect just the way you are.

Most importantly, remember, you are not alone.

CHAPTER SEVEN

Who and what you are.

If you were a flower, what flower would you be?
What colour petals would your flower have?
What is it about this flower that draws your attention?
How would being a flower make you feel?

Hi teen girl!

This is going to be a conversation about **WHO AND WHAT YOU ARE.**

First, pretend you are a flower. A four-petalled flower. Before you carry on reading, please get some coloured pencils so we can play along with this idea.

You will see below my 'Living Flower.' It is the **metaphor** I will use to help you **inner-stand** yourself and gain more knowledge and insight which is what self-awareness is all about.

Now that you have your pencils, lightly shade the centre of the flower using your favourite colour and in capital letters write the word **SELF** using the same colour. Then shade each petal as suggested below:

1. Red (south-facing - petal point downwards)
2. Blue (west - left)
3. Green (east - right)
4. Purple (north - upwards)

You are probably wondering what is this all about? What does a flower have to do with '**SELF-AWARENESS**' and what does self-awareness have to do with what you experience in life? Well, a long time ago, a **philosopher** - *if you do not know what a philosopher is please refer to the* glossary at the end of this chapter - by the name of Aristotle suggested that '*The whole is greater than the sum of all its parts.*'

Look at the different parts of a flower. There is the centre, which is called the **pistil,** the petals, the stem, the leaves, and the roots. There is much more to a flower than the sum of all its parts. There is perfume to it, there is beauty and an essence.

The same goes for you! As a human being, you are much more than the combination of all your body parts! You too have an essence, a personality; intelligence; a story to tell; you are unique, special, and full of potential. You are creative, sensitive, and incredibly powerful! You are so much more than you believe yourSELF to be.

Let's carry on with our game while we explore who you are as a human being, and how being aware of all the **dimensions** that you navigate your life with, can assist you in dealing with life's experiences.

You have already labelled SELF in the centre of the flower. Now please write these four different human dimensions described below:

1. The red petal is your BODY (write body using a red pen and do the same with the other petals).
2. The blue represents your MIND.

3. The green your EMOTIONS.
4. And the purple, your SOUL.

Next, you will find a blank page and I invite you to draw a similar four-petalled flower only this time all in red including its centre. Be sure to draw it big enough using the whole page so that you can label it afterwards.

I HAVE A BODY AND I NEED MY BODY TO EXPERIENCE LIFE AS A HUMAN BEING

THE BODY:

What does your body need in order to develop, grow, and maintain physical health?

Before I give you the answers, I would like you to jot down, at the bottom of the previous page, four things you think our bodies need to work well. This is not a test! Remember, we are just playing a game.

Obviously, we need air to breathe to stay alive. That's a given, right? Then, the most obvious things our bodies need are food and water. Let's call that *nutrition*. Write nutrition on one of the red petals.

Another requirement for the body to maintain its health is sleep and relaxation. Let's call this *rest* and write rest on another petal.

The third one is any form of physical activity. Let's call it *movement - you know what to do!*

The last one is *warmth*. An essential aspect for our growth and development which includes being held from the moment we are born; sheltered from the elements in the natural environment; lovingly caressed by our caregivers and the people we love.

Remember, these are only the most important things that our bodies need to survive. We are also meant to grow, prosper, and thrive.

Feel free to write down everything else you feel your body benefits from including a lovely hot bubble bath with scented candles.

You know the drill now so please draw a blue flower on the next blank page:

I USE MY MIND TO CREATE MY REALITY

THE MIND:

Although every single 'part' of a human life is very important, the 'mind' is like a **portal** that bridges who to what you are. Think about this for a moment: The WHO of a Human being has to do with your personality and the WHAT has to do with our original **blueprint.** Call it our **SOURCE.**

Life is a journey and we need a map to help us navigate it to the best of our abilities.

What do YOU believe you can use your mind for? Write everything that comes to 'mind' at the bottom of your blue flower. Be creative and remember, there is no right or wrong here. It is YOUR MIND so give it a voice and write everything down before carrying on to the next paragraph.

There is a great deal to be said about our minds and its ability to help us create and shape our realities. Did you know you have the power to create your own reality? Let's dive into the four main things we can use the mind for.

First, we use our minds to *learn* about the world around us. Not just information or data. We learn everything by being exposed to our environment. When we are exposed to certain information, our brains help us to digest and process that information and this is called thinking. Similar to *think* we also use our minds to *reflect*. We put our thinking 'hat' on when we need to make decisions and problem solve, and our reflecting one when we need to evaluate our performance.

Our minds also have certain needs. For us to enjoy our learning experiences our minds require *stimulus*. So, it is important to entertain our minds with fun stuff, or we will get bored. There is much our minds can do to help us create the life we wish for ourselves. Please label your blue flower with the word 'mind' in the centre, then with the words learn, think, reflect, and stimulate in whichever petals you choose.

Let's turn our attention to our emotions flower.

THE EMOTIONS:

Emotions are **energy** in **motion**! It is mainly through our emotions that we experience life as we engage with the world around us and the people in it.

Like the mind petal, the emotions one is even more complex. Emotions either give you *pleasure* or *pain* which causes you either to feel calm, experiencing a sense of *peace*. Or you can feel *anxious*.

Please write *pleasure* and *pain* on the east and west facing petals, then *peace* facing north and *anxious* facing south. Then create a many-petalled flower of your own with a petal for every emotion you have experienced in your life. Feel free to use different colours for different feelings.

Know that emotions should flow through you. Something you feel rather than who you are. Pay attention to how you engage with your feelings and avoid identifying yourself with them. For instance, never say "I am sad." Instead, train your mind - *and here is a tip on how you use your mind to create your reality* - to say or think "I feel sadness." Emotions are meant to be felt and experienced. It is NOT who you are so be mindful to avoid identifying yourself with emotions that cause you pain.

Emotions help us become resilient so do not be afraid to feel them. Since emotions are energy in motion they are not supposed to get 'stuck' in your body or in your mind. If they do, it can become overwhelming. Talk to someone if you need help. Asking for help is a sign of strength, you are not meant to suffer alone.

Use this space to draw your unique emotions flower.

THE SOUL:

Okay Goddess Girl, you know the drill. Go ahead and draw your purple flower and write down a few words that you would consider a soul to be.

Let's look at the word SOUL as an acronym:

> **S** stands for *'source'*
>
> **O** for *of*
>
> **U** means *unique*
>
> **L** symbolises *light*.
> Source Of Unique Light!

That is what you are; what we all are. We are all unique individuals, but we all come from the original source of all things seen and unseen.

You are a unique spark of the divine light that comes from our source, the Creator or whatever word you feel comfortable with. Go ahead and label your purple flower as described above.

Self-awareness is a life-long journey. The more we learn about who and what we are, the more there is to learn!

When you are experiencing any discomfort, distress, anxiety, or anything else that causes you to feel a certain way, ask yourself:

1. Where is this feeling coming from? Does it have anything to do with how I relate to my body, my mind, or my emotions?
2. What does this experience relate to? Is it to do with a certain event?
3. How has it come about?
4. And most importantly...
5. What can I do about it?

It is essential for you to realise you are more powerful than what happens to you in life. Your power comes from being *self-aware* enough to challenge your experiences and know that you are stronger than them.

Life is a journey that will lead you to the next best version of yourself should you CHOOSE to. It starts with a decision. You have free will to embrace this journey with excitement and wonder. Mistakes will be made along the way - *WE ALL MAKE THEM!* They will help you develop and grow into the beautiful, elegant, and majestic flowers you are.

Just for fun, I would like you to draw your own unique flower to represent all the different 'petals' of you. I am sharing mine to give you some ideas. Write your name in the centre of the flower then go crazy with your creativity. Be sure to include all the petals you wish to draw for your future **SELF.**

Remember that *"We are Divine beings here on the planet to express our Divinity in human form"* (© Eliana Keen 2020)

Remember teen Goddess:

"Part of what makes a flower beautiful is about how long it takes for it to grow".

(From the Disney film Star Girl based on the novel bearing the same name by Jerry Spinelli)

CHAPTER EIGHT

The Bridge Between

Hello gorgeous! Gosh don't you think there are so many things to think about at once sometimes? Like who really is your best friend, how many of your closest pals have your back or even what on earth are your parents thinking about half the time? I know that this time of your life can feel so confusing. One minute you feel you have found your friend for life and all things are going well then boom, something just comes right out of nowhere and knocks you for six, making you feel like you are back at square one. Well, if that's where you're at right now, please know it's perfectly normal. It's normal to feel confused, concerned and disconnected from those around you from time to time and, hopefully, after you've read this chapter, you will know why.

Firstly, your brain is doing some crazy stuff right now. Your brain's engine house is rebooting and updating some software just like you regularly do with your phone. It's deciding what's important, what's useful and what you need more of in order to thrive as you go through this crazy journey called life. I'm sure you can imagine if your old phone never, ever updated it would take so long to do even the simplest task? Well, your own brain is exactly like that. So, whilst your decision making, problem solving, 'who on earth am I' part of your brain is offline updating itself, you are left with the emotional part of your brain doing all the heavy work. This might help you understand why you feel so overwhelmed with emotions a lot of the time.

Oh, and let's not forget your hormones! Those chemical messengers that surge around your body that not only help it to perform essential functions like breathing but also create some fluctuations in how you feel when your period comes along. I'm sure you'll know yourself that every month there are times when you feel different in your body and mind and you may even make decisions that come from a whole different part of you than usual. Our hormones can have such an overwhelming effect on us at times you may even question who's in charge here? Oh, the joys of being female!

So, if that's the human body bit covered off, what about your emotional and mental wellbeing and why is this chapter called The Bridge Between? Well, beautiful, as you are going through the most amazing changes in your life right now, I know it can feel so overwhelming at times you don't know who YOU are. Even if you feel able to turn to friends, family, teachers, coaches to talk to them about how you are feeling, it does not stop you from sometimes still feeling lost, confused and generally fed up with how life is unfolding. Why is that?

Well, I believe it's because you are going through the stage of your life that is the bridge between the small child who needs things done for them by a caring adult and turning into the adult you were destined to become. It's like a no man's land of change where nothing feels concrete or certain and that bridge can feel so scary when you are walking across it.

As a Mum myself, I am watching with pure admiration in my heart as my 18-year-old daughter matures into the woman of her own choosing. But even though every fibre of my being wants to, I can't cross that bridge with her. If I did that, I would be putting my own thoughts, feelings and desires on to her path, possibly influencing her decisions and impacting on her own feelings of self-worth and ability to make the choices that SHE wants to. But gosh how I want to go with her on that bridge. To protect her from the harshness of life, to protect her from other's viewpoints and to protect her heart from being hurt. You see I remember being that 18-year-old myself, forging ahead into my life not knowing who I was really deep down inside. Yes, I had a job that took me well out of my comfort zone, but it also created an awkwardness inside me as I tried to conform to societies expectations of who I should be. But my experience and journey are not what is destined for my own child in the same way that any adult who is in your life can't decide who YOU are. Only you can do that.

As you grow into the adult you were destined to become there are many things you may wish to think about on the bridge. It's a good time to reflect on what you do know about yourself. Even though the decision-making and problem-solving part of your brain is offline for a large part of your teenage years, it doesn't mean you stop learning about your SELF. Somewhere deep down inside is the SELF. The deepest, tiniest, purest dot of pure energy that has been there since you were born. It's the part of you that never changes. It's the part of you that has been there through your ups and downs and roundabouts. It's like beacon of white light that often gets covered up by your early life experiences and you learn to hide for fear of being seen. So firstly, I want you to connect with that part of you, the part that seems to already know which direction you are going in and take a moment to remind yourself of what you know. Take time to connect with your own innate skills and abilities that you already have. What comes easy to you? When do you feel most able? When do you feel most like YOU? Is it when you are gaming, doing a sport, a hobby, talking with your friends, doing your job or even reading a book and doing a review online? It could be absolutely anything. So even though it may take you some time, you WILL have positive things to write down that you know about yourself. So go write down some statements around I love to….. I can…., I am able to…., I find…. easy to do. Perhaps even set yourself a timer for 10 minutes and just write? It's such a beautiful exercise to do as it reminds you of who YOU are amongst all the noise.

Whilst you are still on the bridge between, you may also want to think about the experiences that have led you to where you are now. Some of those experiences may be unpleasant and wish had never happened, but some will be beautiful memories that you wish never stopped. As you reflect on those memories ask yourself – what did I learn about ME at that time? Even in the most horrible situations you can learn something positive about who you are, your values and what you care about. I believe that through the roughest of times you can learn that you are tough, resilient and CAN still get up every day and persevere. If life has been hard for you up until this point, please know you are already brilliant, capable, resourceful, loved and worthy. Those events are not a rod to hold you back but fuel to ignite that fire inside your belly to keep going. You will know yourself more because of those things so please don't allow them to dampen who you believe you should be. Scientific research actually shows us that early life experiences can create the most amazing leaders that the world needs so rather thinking I cannot do this thing I want to because of what I believe I experienced, think I CAN do it because of what I've gone through. Let it be the fuel that carries you through.

Now I'd like to speak to you about your parents or the caregivers who have influenced your life and their desire to come over that bridge with you! The pull for them will be very real because they will want to protect you and save you from any harm. It's a such an unconscious and natural thing for a parent to want to protect but actually, for you, it can feel like suffocation. It can feel like you have no space to BE yourself and express who you really are without any external influence to conform to. One thing I'd ask you to consider is your parent's own stories of their childhood and how that might influence their desires for your life. Personally, when I left school at 16, I really wanted to be ballet teacher but was 'encouraged' to leave school to walk into an office junior job. It literally broke my heart not to follow my dream, but I never spoke up. I never told any living soul what was crying out inside of me at the time. I often wonder how my life would have unfolded had I listened to that inner calling inside of me and learned how to speak up. Even though I was 16 I allowed my parents to influence me so greatly that I stopped following my passion – I even gave up dancing at age 18. To be clear my parents loved me and loved me so much they didn't want me to fail in any way. To them coming out of school straight into a job was a huge success and something to be very proud of. But it wasn't my dream. However, from my personal experience, I learned that I cannot even be on the bridge with my own daughter. I do not want to stifle her own discovery of what lies ahead because, it's through that journey over the bridge, that she will confirm her strengths and be led by her own inner shining star. Not mine.

So, as you make your own way over the bridge, you have the opportunity to learn so much about yourself. It's perfectly OK to feel unsure of the way ahead because you are moving forward with less influence from others. If you feel the pull towards your friends and away from your parents, it may be because your parents are struggling not being able to join you on the bridge? It could be you can relate more to your friends at this time because they too are making their way over the bridge towards the adult they want to become. And that's perfectly ok. It's also perfectly OK to ask for the space to grow. If you are feeling constricted and held back from making your own decisions, it's ok to say that's how you feel. I know that, as parents, we want our kids to grow up able to deal with conflict, think independently and how to bounce back from knock backs. But if you are unable to walk that bridge by yourself, how will you learn that you can face the experiences that will allow you to grow in this way.

Being a parent isn't easy. Adults do not have all their stuff together and truth be told we're all just learning how to do this stuff as it comes up. And being vulnerable in front of our kids is hard so if some of your conversations have been a bit prickly up until this point it might help you to understand it's not because you are not an amazing and worthy daughter. It could be that you parents don't know about the bridge between.

I truly believe that you, my gorgeous one, are your parents' biggest teacher. You have such an amazing ability to help the adults around you grow and learn from the shining star that you are. So please know that by you finding your own voice and ability to speak up it will not only help you on your journey but also your family and friends and everyone around you. Now, as you find your own way across your bridge between and rediscover your inner guiding light, you realise it's always been there. Yeh, it might have got a bit covered up with unnecessary stuff, but you now remember it's never moved away from where it all began. It will always be there helping you light the way across the bridge between. It's somehow already knows which way to go.

CHAPTER NINE

Becoming

Coming of age is a term that I always despised as a teenager. I remember people commenting, saying things like, 'Oh, she is really coming of age, isn't she?'. I mean what the heck did that mean? Coming of age. As if at any moment some age switch was going to flip! Providing me with... like I had any idea!

Now, some 30 plus years later, I understand the phrase better. But even though I understand that what they are referring to is the age of becoming independent, I still cringe every time I hear it. Personally, I prefer the phrase 'becoming'.

What does 'becoming' mean?

To become; the process of coming to be something or of passing into a new state.

But what is it that we are becoming? Rather, what is it that *you* are becoming?

Truthfully, that is 100% up to you. I hope that reading this chapter you are able to have some fun, gather some tools, and, before you flip to the next chapter, feel that you know who you, yes *YOU*, are becoming!

To begin, you must first ask, 'Who am I?'. So, who are you?
Before you answer let me tell you who you are NOT.
You are not your mom, mommy, mama, mother, Ima, or mum.
You are not your dad, daddy, papa, father, Abba, pop.
You are not your sister, your brother, your cousin, or your best friend.

No matter how many times someone tells you that you are just like so and so, you are not.

You, my friend, are you. A unique, beautiful, perfect being. There is no other mold that is identical to yours. This is Truth.

Now that we have established who you are not and that it is Truth, you are probably wondering what I mean by Truth. I am talking about Universal Truth. The Truth of all Truths. That we are all connected in one collective. A lot, right? It can seem to be at the start. But I promise it is not. Universal Truth is just that, truth that cannot be disputed.

Relative truth is the truth formed from each individual's perspective. You know the kind. Perhaps, you do not respond to your parent immediately; taking time to consider your answer. Thinking to yourself; "Don't they always tell me to think before I speak, anyway?" But then they get upset with you for ignoring them.

Has this or something similar ever happened to you? The conversation might look something like this:

Parent says: "Answer me!" or "Don't ignore me when I am speaking to you." Or even "Are you giving me attitude?".

You reply: "I am not ignoring you; I just don't know."

Then they come back with: "Don't lie to me." or "Then why didn't you answer?"

You may feel attacked, and know you were not ignoring your parent. That is *your* relative truth. On the other hand, your parent may know that you DID ignore them, because you plainly did not answer. That is their truth, their relative truth.

The Universal Truth is the Absolute Truth. The Universal Truth is that both you and your parent, in this example, are eternal beings who are reflecting upon one another. The Universal Truth reveals this, reveals we are one collective, sharing memories and experiences.

Is your mind blown yet? It blew mine the first time I began to understand. Let me explain it this way:

Have you ever been around someone sad, or seen something sad, and immediately felt sad along with that person, regardless of whether you know them or not?

Have you ever seen a marriage proposal and felt a surge of joy and emotion even though you are not old enough to be married or thinking about marriage?

I found this so confusing before I understood that the Universal Truth is that we are *all* connected, one collective. Once we know this, we can understand why it is so important to be clear about who you are becoming. We feel and experience as the Universal Collective. Therefore, we need to understand who we are. The I AM.

So, who are you becoming?

That is a BIG question, I know.

When Deliah was 15, she did not know who she was becoming. She had had the same group of friends from childhood. They coordinated their outfits, daily. They shared their most intimate secret crushes and supported one another when their family and home life was not all they wanted.

Deliah's family was a big one. She had three brothers and one sister. They bickered, but for the most part, everyone got along. Her parents listened to her when she thought differently and sometimes even saw things from her point of view. Even changed their minds about some things when she explained to them from her relative truth/ perspective.

Deliah felt that she had the ability, support and a nurturing environment that would allow her to become, allowing her to feel as if she is twirling through a ballet of her own choreographing.

She is clear on who she is becoming, she sees a path through the space she has been given to observe herself and knows the Truth of the I Am within her.

Yurit, on the other hand, came from a two-person household. She lived with her grandfather. He loved her; she knew this. He worked a lot and was very old-fashioned but allowed Yurit to grow and teach him new things. He gave her a curfew and celebrated every good mark from school with her. She lived to please her hard-working grandfather.

Yurit would spend weekends studying and overachieving so she could live up to everything she felt her grandfather wanted. Her grandfather encouraged her to have friends and to do more of the things she loved. She would smile and hug him, say thank you, and go back to studying. Even though he did this, and expressed his pride and love for Yurit, she could not see a path to Truth and had lost touch with her I Am.

She created a chasm or gap from Truth. Their circumstances were far from dire, and she was aware of that. It was her grandfather's pride in her, her wanting to please him and her fear of disapproval from him, that kept her disconnected from the I AM.

What was the main difference between these two girls and their Truths? Was it their circumstances? Their family dynamics? Perhaps, all of that came into play. But Truth is Truth and connecting to the I Am in each of us is the key to understanding it.

Did Yurit's grandfather cause her to become something she did not want to be? He most definitely did not, he only ever expressed love and pride to her. It was her own consciousness that caused the rift between her and Truth. So how could Yurit reconnect with her I Am?

How can *you* connect to your I Am and Truth?

Through celebration of course!! No, I am not joking. Celebrating makes us smile, reminds us that we have a reason to be happy, to be alive, to... CELEBRATE!

Let's begin right now!

I love to use a technique called visualization. Many of you may have made a vision board or two. This is not that. I do love me some vision boards though!

Let's explore visualization together: I want you to complete the activity below:

I AM VISUALIZATION:

1. Find a comfortable space somewhere. Settle in with a pen and paper, a journal, a phone, or other device to record your story.

2. Close your eyes. Inhale through your nose, pausing at the top of the breath, take another sippy breath of air and with an audible "HAAAAAAAAAHHHHH" exhale. Repeat this 3 times. Then sit quietly for a few moments.

3. As you sit quietly, I want you to let your mind wander to a time when you wanted to say who you were to someone. Connect with your I AM. Now is that time. Make the declarations below, either by speaking them or writing them down.

4. Place your right hand over your heart and say I Am Me...and any other I Am's you feel coming up. Trust yourself.

    For example. "I AM me. I AM smart and I AM beautiful. I AM understanding. I AM Hearing you and I AM Heard. I AM Loved. I AM Worthy of love. I AM worthy of friends. I AM worthy."

5. Now, hold your left hand out in front of you. Say to that person, the same things you said to yourself.

    For Example. "YOU Are you. YOU Are smart and YOU Are beautiful. YOU Are understanding. YOU Are Hearing me, and

YOU Are Heard. YOU Are Loved. YOU Are Worthy of love. YOU Are worthy of friends. YOU Are worthy."

How do you feel now? Can you feel the I AM that is you? The I AM that is them? By covering your heart, you are recognizing in love to be honoured, that you are, in fact WORTHY.

By holding up your other hand you are honouring the other person, accepting without judgement who they are. Spreading and connecting your love from your heart and sending it to them while remaining true to yourself. Truth.

★TIP★ I love music, so I often have music to celebrate the I AM that is me when I give thanks after Visualization.

This is BECOMING. This is how you can discover your I AM. Use this handy visualization tool any time you feel that you are losing the becoming of the I Am that is you.

As we reach the end of this chapter, I want each and every reader to know that I see and visualize Truth for you. I am holding a safe space for each Girl Goddess to feel becoming. To celebrate! A coming out of sorts. The coming out of the I AM in each of you Girl Goddesses.

That is the space and the visualization that I see. For every Girl Goddess to know Universal Truth and feel the connection to her very own and unique I AM.

So now, CELEBRATE!! Giving thanks for Truth for life. Giving Thanks and celebrating YOU! YOU ARE BECOMING.

The I AM that is YOU. Then...dance baby dance!

CHAPTER TEN

Honour how you feel.

Hey girl!

I see you!
I see you putting on that brave face.
I see you pretending everything is ok.

I see the girl whose world got turned upside down the day you found out your mom had Cancer.

At that moment, your life changed. You were no longer just you. A teenage girl, living what was supposed to be her best years. These next few years were supposed to be when you discover who you are. You should have been living life to the fullest and making memories that would last a lifetime. After all, your teenage years are the years that great movies are made about. But the script to your movie just had a dramatic re-write!

You are now in the starring role of a teenage girl whose mom has Cancer.

Fear, sadness and worry come flooding in. Your feelings are so out of control, they begin to take over your mind. Your brain kicks into overdrive and your focus is no longer on the great party that was happening tonight. It is about 'will my mom die while I am at the party?' How will we survive if she dies? Will I get cancer?

You tell yourself, 'This is not going to change my life. It is not going to change anything because it is not happening to me. I am not the one with Cancer'.

As time passes, the reality sets in that things have changed. Cancer does not just affect the one diagnosed. It affects everyone around them. Especially when it is someone so close to you.

I see your mind spinning as you discover not everyone wants to know the truth. At first, you are completely honest with people when they ask, 'how's your mom doing?' You open your heart and tell them the honest truth. 'It's not great', you say.

You tell them about all the treatments and the side effects. You talk about the nurses and the sleepless nights. But then you notice how people react. You see a shocked expression on their faces as they realize how bad it is. They may change the topic or downplay the severity of the situation. You quickly learn that not everyone wants to know the truth. So, you begin to hide the truth, hide your feelings because you do not want to make anyone feel uncomfortable.

I see the fake smile you wear every day. Always putting a positive spin on things to protect someone else's feelings, while neglecting your own. It is exhausting. Pretending life is normal and that everything is ok for the sole purpose of not making other people uncomfortable. When you are drowning in your feelings, and you just need someone to make all this misery go away.

I see the neglect from your parents. Once you were the center of their attention. Now it feels like they do not even know you exist. The only time they acknowledge you is when there is something they need. Their focus is not on you. You understand why but you still feel alone. You feel sad, unloved.

You hide. Laying in your bed, under your covers. Grateful for the weight of the blanket, that feels like a hug. Providing protection from the reality of your world.

I see you slowly changing. I see you trying to be on your best behavior to make life easier for your family. I see you doing your part to help out by keeping the house tidy. Cleaning the dishes, sweeping the floor. Or taking out the garbage that has been sitting in the garage for weeks, because no one remembers what day of the week it is.

I see you making dinner so both your parents can catch a few extra minutes of much-needed rest. Some days you feel glad that you can help; that it is your responsibility to help out with these household duties. But other days it feels like such a burden. A teenager, who should be focused on herself now finds herself mimicking the behaviors of a grown woman, taking care of her family.

Living a life that is well beyond her years. Living the life of an adult.

I see what used to be your home, feeling like a hospital, with strict rules for washing hands and limiting visitors. Your home is no longer a home. What used to be filled with laughter and love, is now quiet. Either someone is napping, or loud noises are too much for your mom to bear.

The quiet makes it difficult to release your feelings when the sadness gets too much. You find a safe space within the shower. The sound of the water helps drown out your cries. Your tears release with so much force it drops you to your knees and you sit there, curled up in the bottom of the shower, allowing the stream of water to gather your tears and flow down the drain.

I see you having conversations with your parents. You look at them closely. They are putting on a brave face, as they give you the latest updates from the doctors. However, the tears in their eyes do not match the words they speak.

I hear the thoughts running through your head, 'I can handle this.' 'I need to know.' 'Are they hiding something from me', 'I wish they wouldn't try to protect me.' But you are doing the same thing, trying to protect them. You do everything in your power to be on your best behavior because you do not want to cause your family any more stress. The pressure of being so perfect all the time is hard and exhausting.

This behavior is hard to maintain. It is hard to keep up this version of yourself. The version that you feel everyone expects you to be. You are not a child, but you are also not an adult yet.

But you are expected to deal with adult situations while still feeling like 'this is all too heavy for someone my age to deal with'.

The stress, worry and tension of all of it starts to take its toll on your family. The family which used to be loving and fun is now short and snappy. What used to make them smile, now frustrates them. The fun times feel like a lifetime ago and there is no telling when you may be able to start making memories and having fun again.

I see you struggle to focus at school when all you can think of is what is happening at home. It is treatment day. Is everything going to be ok? I wonder how they are feeling. You are supposed to focus and learn but every time you look at your book, your mind goes blank. You cannot retain any of this information because it does not seem important. You cannot focus, you cannot be alone with your thoughts.

I see you struggling to stay present. I see you rushing to turn on Netflix to drown out your thoughts. I see you snapping your friends with filters, so they do not see the real pain in your eyes.

I see you feeling selfish for thinking of yourself. This is not supposed to be about you. It is about your mom. But you are dealing with this too. This affects you as well and this is some heavy stuff! This has changed your life in a way you did not want. Why did this happen to your family? This has caused you to be a person who is anxious and sad. This is not you. This is not how life is supposed to be.

I see you feeling confused, watching some of your friends stick around and others fade away. At first, everyone is so supportive. They send texts and video chat, telling you how they will support you and that you are not alone. But as the months pass, they are not as eager to answer your texts.

I see the sadness when the friends you thought would have your back, be your ride or die, no longer know what to say to you. They no longer want to be around you because they are not able to handle hearing about everything you are going through. They want to keep it fun and light, talk about normal teenage things, not your feelings. This makes you sad because all you were looking for was some support from your friends.

But then there are the friends who do step up and support you, no matter what. They are there to make you smile or pass you a tissue when you just cannot hold back the tears. They are there to agree with you that this sucks and do whatever they can to support you. They are your real earth angels. You know this is true friendship and will last a lifetime.

I see the fear of missing out you feel when you see your friends post pictures and stories. They are having fun without a care in the world. You grieve the life you once had, as you stay home, helping out your family. You question when will things go back to normal?

Even when you do go out and try to forget about what is going on at home, you are never really present. You may be able to get away and have a few hours of freedom, of what makes you feel normal, but when you walk through the doors of your house, it hits you in the face that this is your reality. This is your new normal.

You hear people tell you how strong you are, but what does that even mean? When you look a certain way on the outside but are crying, kicking, and screaming on the inside? Strong is the furthest of what you feel.

I could spend the rest of our time together telling you to stay positive or maybe you should try this technique to help you feel better, but I am not going to do that.

The last thing you want right now is someone adding one more thing for you to do, to your already full plate.

What I can do, is provide you with a space where you can be completely honest and let go of the fears of being judged or saying the wrong thing.

This is about you and no one else right now.

This is your journey, your feelings, your experience.

Your feelings are yours, and they are powerful, and they deserve to be acknowledged.

Life is not always about looking for a positive spin on things.
Sometimes it is just about the acknowledgement of what you are feeling.
Understanding that you are not alone.
That what you are feeling, someone else has felt it too
That someone else understands you.

I am not here to tell you what to do
or to say things will get better
I am meeting you where you are at
In this moment of struggle.
Through this hard stuff!
Because let's face it, it is so hard.

You are seen, you are heard, you are understood.
You are being reminded that your feelings matter because they do
Here, in this moment, you are not judged or told to put on a happy face.
You are supported no matter what you are feeling.

This is about honoring you, a beautiful spirit who is experiencing some really hard stuff.

I hold a space for you in my heart and on the pages of this book.
I honor your feelings because your feelings matter.
No one can take those away from you
No one can tell you how to feel
They are your own thoughts from your heart.
They are raw, they are painful, they hold energy.
And people may not be able to understand them,
They may even try to dismiss them,
But you, my goddess, my girl,
Are far more advanced when it comes to being in touch with your emotions
And are free to express them here.

You do not have to pretend anymore
You know your feelings matter.
You know your feelings are valid.
You know it is safe to be vulnerable and open your heart and express
how you feel
You know you will not be judged or disciplined.

You will be seen, felt, and heard
What I am saying is…

Hey girl,
I see you.
I see you putting on that brave face.
I see you pretending everything is ok.

CHAPTER ELEVEN

The masks I wore

Meet the feisty, high-achieving fun girl who jokes in class, excels at sports and loves being part of a team; the one who has lots of friends and is always out and about having a laugh.

That's me, Lisa. I am 15 years old.

But look a little deeper and you will see what I am desperately covering up. At home and in my life. Years of domestic violence that I see, feel, and hear. The sexual assault when I was 12. My drinking and drug-taking. The shoplifting. My rapidly snowballing lack of self-respect leading to increased risky and promiscuous situations.

Three and half decades later…and I am wondering how I got through all of that to be celebrating my 50th birthday this year. Yes, I can hear you thinking 'OMG you are older than my mum'. I get it. It took me a while to sort my life out.

My reason for sharing my story with you is to show you it can be done. That you can survive bad stuff and find a better life.

Maybe life is hard right now, and you cannot imagine it ever being different. I hope my story shows you that thing can get better.

One thing though, please do not leave it 30 years to sort it out as I did.

No matter how you are feeling; whatever challenges you are facing; there are ways to get support and help out there. But if it is not possible for you to access help right now (for any number of reasons), I have some suggestions that may help you.

Throughout my childhood and my teenage years, I created masks to wear to help me deal with the daily challenges I faced. I did not even know I was doing it.

I wore different masks at different times.

There was the Joker mask. This one was to hide the fact that despite the unconditional love that Mum gave to my brother and me, life often felt scary.

This mask helped me to live a double life so that no one would know or ever guess what was really going on. If I were the 'The joker' nobody would ever think I was sad or needed connection, meaning that nobody would ask me, 'Are you alright?'

The next one was the Lone Ranger mask. 'I can do it myself', 'I don't need anyone'.

The trouble was, I did not trust anyone.

As a result of all this, I made sure nobody got close to me, especially in relationships. 'How could I trust anyone with my heart again'.

Then there was the People Pleaser Mask. Where do I start with this one?

This is the mask I wore most often. It is also the one that I have had the greatest pleasure taking off. Always helping others. Giving up my time, my energy, my money, my self-worth and so much more.

Being kind and helpful is one thing. But when it is causing you more harm than good, then you need to check-in and remember to look after yourself too. I had no boundaries and would often put my own health on the line.

The masks were very important to me when I was growing up. I really needed them. They were my comfort blanket, they kept me safe, they helped me cope.

But as I got older, they began to have a big negative impact on my life. I felt like I was not being true to myself. I was not letting anyone near even though I desperately wanted that closeness. I was constantly exhausted from being there for everyone else, all of the time. But I did not know how to be there for myself. I knew something had to change.

What I am trying to explain may not make sense right now. It may seem confusing. I know I could not understand it when I was in the middle of it all. Looking back now, I can see clearly what was happening. It looks obvious.

It is as though my older self is watching a play starring my younger self. From my seat in the theatre, I can see all the different characters and how they act and interact. I see and hear what the other characters want little Lisa to see and believe. I watch myself taking my masks on and off. Hiding my true self.

Stepping out of the play of my life, sitting back, and observing, gave me the space to take it all in. To view things from all perspectives. To figure out how things had happened. Helped me understand what it meant, what it did not mean and how that could help me make sense of it all.

As a child and teenager, I never had an opportunity to step out of the play of my life. But as I grew older, I took more time to sit in the audience and watch what was happening. That is when it all started to make sense.

Back then, if you had asked me what was actually going on for me, I would not have been able to tell you. I did not even know the masks existed, so how could I have explained why I wore them? But on reflection, I know that I was doing the very best that I could to survive and cope with everything that was happening.

And so are you. You are doing a great job right now! You are doing the very best that you can.

Here are a few things I have done to help myself when things were challenging. If you think they may help you, I would love you to try them.

They spell out the word S.E.L.F.L.O.V.E

Because once I understood that I am loveable as the unique person that I am and that there is no one else the same as me - that is when I knew my journey to loving Lisa could begin and I started to re-connect to me.

I hope this helps

S is for Stress

Stress affects us in so many ways, from stopping us from sleeping, skin problems, weight issues, anxiety; to name but a few.

Ask yourself:

'What is causing me stress?'

Becoming aware; identifying the situations, people, places, and environments that were the trigger of my stress was key.

'How can I ease or take away that stress?'

Recognising the stress and then discovering how to manage it, reduce it, or stop it changed everything. In addition to this, putting systems in place to keep on top of my stress levels helped to stop the stress from building up again.

E is for Environment

Our environment has a huge impact on us. If we are surrounded by negativity, it can make us unhappy or even make us feel physically unwell. It might be a messy space; being around people that we do not want to spend time with or doing things we do not want to do.

One of the ways I helped myself was to spend less time with people I could not be my true self around. I wanted to be me. And I stopped going to places I did not want to go to. I practised asking myself, '*Do I want to go there right now*', or '*Do I want to spend time with those people at the moment?*'.

It did not mean that I would never go again, it just meant that I needed to put myself first at that time.

L is for Language

There were times I would say very negative things to myself.

'*I can't do…*', '*I'm not good enough to do…*', '*I don't deserve…*'.

I would never say these things about other people, but I was saying them about myself.

One of the most impactful things I did to change my negative self-talk habit was to do positive affirmations every day.

It felt uncomfortable at first, so I started with simple things like,

'I am doing the very best I can to…', 'I can do…'.

As I became more comfortable with saying these things, I progressed to more powerful statements that all started with I AM…

F is for Focus

When we focus on being truly present in the moment it helps us feel less depressed about the past and less anxious about what the future may hold. Because we cannot be in the past, the present and the future all at the same time. Learning to be present, right here, right now was powerful for me.

Try this: Get comfortable, sitting or standing and using all your senses, look around you. Describe what you can see, what you can smell, what you can hear, what you can feel and even what you can taste in minute detail, it is amazing how your mind cannot wander when it is focused.

L is for Lessons

I am not asking you to study, I promise!

I am talking about learning lessons from things that keep happening. Things you know you would like to change.

It could be something simple like changing an unhealthy habit because it makes you feel rubbish. Or getting more sleep because you are struggling to get up in the morning and it takes you ages to wake up. Or maybe you do not like the way someone speaks to you. You want to change it because it keeps happening and it is affecting you.

Become aware of which patterns keep repeating.
Note how the particular issue is making you feel.
What can you do that will make the situation better?
How will you feel once you have created that change?

Then you can attach a positive feeling to the change and can see it is possible.

O is for Opportunities

Opportunities is all about being curious. Trying new things. Grabbing opportunities to grow, learn and have fun.

What have you always wanted to do but never started?
What would you like to try?

Every expert was once a beginner. Take every opportunity to expand your knowledge. Learn new skills. Have fun in a different way.

If it feels uncomfortable at first, keep going, confidence is a skill that we develop, like a muscle. The more you do, the stronger it gets!

<u>*V is for Vulnerability*</u>

This was one of the hardest ones for me. I saw vulnerability as a weakness. I always thought I needed to be strong. I could do it myself. Remember the Lone Ranger Mask?

I did this one step at a time. Sharing what I was happy with someone I knew I could trust. A little at a time. One step at a time. There are always people who can support and help you.

<u>*E is for Expectations*</u>

We put so much pressure on ourselves trying to live up to expectations. Our own, or other peoples. This can be very challenging.

One of the ways I helped myself was to practice some self-compassion.

I reminded myself every day, that I was doing the best that I could do.

Some days were better than others, and on the days that were not so good I would tell myself

"I am doing the best that I can today and that is enough".

I hope that this helps you take off your masks!

CHAPTER TWELVE

Shine so bright, they will need shades!

I was thirteen years old. Excited and happy to be competing in a swim meet, near some of my family, who had never come to watch me swim before. I had been working very hard; two practices a day, lifting weights, dryland workouts, and running. All the things needed to establish the right mindset to become a champion swimmer.

I was feeling proud of myself. Because after all the long hours and sacrifice, I was experiencing a rapid improvement in my abilities and my success. Like the bamboo tree, which takes 5 years to grow its roots but then shoots up 3 feet in 24 hours, I was finally riding the waves of growth and success.

I swam many events that day and even won a few. I placed in the top 8 in others and swam all personal best times. I did not get to see much of my family except through the spectator's fence when they gave me a little wave and a thumbs up.

When my races and relays were over, I could finally get some French fries. I don't eat very much when I race, as I tend to be nervous and that means I spend too much time in the bathroom. OK! Maybe too much information!

Anyway, I headed over to see my mom, aunt, uncle, and cousins.

Nibbling on my fries with ketchup, I walked over to my family. Mom hugged me, telling me how proud she was. My aunt and uncle were blown away by how good I had become. They also told me how proud they were of me. One of my cousins was excited to see me. She hugged me too and told me she was happy for me. She knew how hard I had been working.

Then it happened. Two of my other cousins did not even speak to me. They turned away, ignoring me, giving me the cold shoulder. I was confused. I did not understand what was happening. So many people celebrating with me, but I was feeling rejected at the same time.

At that moment, I made a decision. A subconscious decision. That it is best not to be 'too good'. People, even people you love, even your family, will reject you. They will feel bad, and they will make you feel bad too.

Be successful, but not too successful. Be good, but not too good. Be the best, but not really.

These beliefs stayed with me for over 50 years.

Buried in my subconscious mind. Like a computer program running my life. Every time I was successful or allowed myself to 'shine', I would stop myself celebrating. Or I would sabotage myself (we do not do this on purpose) to avoid being successful. By getting sick or hurt. By worrying, judging, and criticizing (myself or others). By blaming and shaming.

A few years later, it began to look like my dream of swimming in the 1980 Olympics was coming true. I had been ranked 15th in the world in the 200 freestyle.

Guess what? I developed an eating disorder (anorexia, then bulimia). I had a shoulder injury, and 6 months out from the Olympic trials I got sick with a bad case of pneumonia.

There were many things going on. Political and personal. The U.S. decided to boycott the 1980 Olympics. But then there was one big personal issue that created a lot of distress for me.

I met my biological father for the first time.

That experience convinced me that I was not worthy. Not good enough; not lovable enough. These beliefs were added to the others I had already embraced; do not

be too good; do not shine too brightly. Together they created a perfect storm.

I never made it to the Olympic trials. My parents had financial problems, so we could not afford it, and I was struggling with illness and injury. It was sad that my Olympic dream had fallen apart, but what was more devastating, was what happened to my belief in myself.

Throughout my senior year in high school, I struggled. With my identity, my self-worth, my body image and with being good enough. I gained 70 pounds. I was filled with self-loathing and shame. The truth is I did not even want to take a shower, much less swim. But I continued swimming through my high school season (not competitively), all the while struggling with bulimia, binge, and emotional eating.

With all the trauma and drama going on, I created some new limiting beliefs: I am not the right size, I am not worthy of success, success is not for me. It does not matter how hard I work, things do not work out for me, I don't fit in, I have to change myself to fit in.

I hope you can see how the 'stories' I was believing about myself were keeping me stuck. No amount of 'positive thinking' was going to get me through this. And being a champion athlete, I knew how to psych myself up. I played ping pong in my mind. Thoughts like, 'you are such a mess', 'You are a loser', 'get your act together', 'you don't have what it takes', would rumble in my head. Along with, 'you are doing the best you can', 'you can do this', and other more compassionate and loving thoughts. In the end, I spent years struggling with my own mind, trying to prove myself worthy, but not feeling worthy, no matter how much success I had.

Decades later, (yes, I said decades!), I would discover that I invested a lot of meaning in all those experiences, and the negative emotions attached to them. I made these 'traumas' or highly unpleasant happenings mean something about me, about other people and about life in general.

The meaning we attach to things that happen in our lives creates our suffering or our happiness. We revisit all the emotions and feelings and continue to energize them by creating stories around them. 'I am not good enough, even my father doesn't want me'.

The good news is it does not have to be that way!

There is an easy way to make powerful shifts in your life, not only now as a young woman, but throughout your entire life. It is as simple as ABC!

A is for Awareness, B is for Beliefs, and C is for Connection.

Awareness is everything. You cannot change something until you are aware of how it is impacting you and your life. Becoming aware of your thoughts and your feelings is the first step to creating the life you were born to live.

Once you learn that you can choose new thoughts and new beliefs (do not believe everything you think) you will experience more joy, more freedom, and more empowerment.

Once you become aware of how the universe actually works. How YOU are the creator of everything, with your imagination, your mind and what you are choosing to energize, you will be unstoppable.

The limiting belief, 'Do not outshine others, because they will feel bad', is so common that I noticed it everywhere.

I noticed it when our son was having some challenges in high school. And when his younger sister began to have illnesses at the start of her own high school swim season.

I noticed when some of the girl swimmers on the team I coached, got jealous and treated their teammate differently when she excelled. When my daughter was treated rudely by another girl when she was faster at practice.

I noticed it with my clients who would want to make their own big leaps but felt paralyzed by their fear of rejection. Just like me.

In his book, The Big Leap, Gay Hendricks, a psychologist, talks about this as an 'upper limit' problem. He calls it, 'The curse of outshining others'. Many gifted and talented people unconsciously sabotage themselves. Like a singer who suddenly loses her voice or gets sick before a big event. An athlete who becomes ill or injured before the big game.

What is great is that now we know this may be just a story that we are believing, we have the power to change it. We can choose a new way to think about what is happening within us instead of saying; 'Well, I guess I am not meant to be an actress/singer/athlete or successful'.

ACTION STEP: One of the easiest ways to find out what you believe is to journal, your thoughts every day. Get it all out on paper and then notice what you notice. With self-love and compassion, you can begin to unpack your own stories.

The 'B' in the ABC's is for **BELIEF**. There is power in questioning your beliefs.

One of my favorite mantras is, 'Do not believe everything you think'.

You need to question your thoughts and beliefs. Most of which are not yours anyway. You inherited them from adults, parents, society, teachers, and your peers. You need to do what is called, 'inner work'.

This is where you use different tools and find different ways to listen to your intuition. To heal old traumas, upsets, parental wounds, and childhood issues.

Journaling, meditation, coaching, therapy, trauma work, art, music, dance. Creative expression of all kinds will help you reconnect to who you are underneath all your stories.

The truth is, you are a powerful creator. You have everything you need within you to be, do and have anything you want. When you wake up to this and truly believe in yourself. When you take full responsibility for your life and what is going on in your mind, You will see your life change.

Change your questions and you change your life. Asking a lot of 'why' questions will only give limited answers. Questions like, 'Why is this happening to me?', 'why are they so mean to me?', or 'why did he break up with me?' will not bring you the answers you are looking for.

Asking better questions is the secret. 'What can I learn from this? What am I really afraid will happen? Who can I reach out to, to help me? What can I do where I am with what I have?'

Ask these types of questions and then journal about the answers that come to you.

C is for **CONNECTION**. The third thing everyone needs is connection and support.

We all need safe, authentic, connections to help us grow, try new things and feel supported, encouraged and loved while doing so. Sometimes our family does not get us. Sometimes we shape-shift to fit in at school.

We all want love and connection (that does not end when you grow up. The best connection you can create is the one with yourself. Learn to love yourself. Learn how you are a divine spiritual being. Learn that you are 'love' and loved.

Connecting with your divine self, the source of all-knowing, all answers and all resources will mean you will never feel alone. You are always connected to this source (whatever you call it, God, Universe) and it is through this connection that you realize you are connected to everyone and everything.

Know that you are perfect, exactly as you are. You are here to live your best life. To shine in whatever way you choose. There is enough room in this universe for all of us to shine.

I hope you will use the ABC's to become aware of your thoughts and choose new ones if you wish. Question your beliefs and let go of those that are not helpful.

Finally, know that creating a connection with yourself (your divine self) is the first step in feeling connected to everyone and everything else.

I give you permission to shine so bright, that they need shades!

CHAPTER THIRTEEN

Resilience and Gratitude

Resilience and gratitude are two fundamentals of my existence.

Resilience and gratitude are all I know.

If you had asked 14-year-old-me if that was what my story was about, I would probably have told you to shove off (only much more colorfully).

For as long as I remember, I have felt 'not enough'.

Not pretty enough.
Not strong enough.
Not smart enough.
Not going to amount to anything.
Nobody will ever love me.

Message after message sounding off in my head. Relentlessly, leaving me feeling limited and burdened. Tentacles of fear that strangled my soul, stealing all my happiness and light.

Despite all of those thoughts churning in my head, I smiled. Acted as if I had no doubt. Kept those voices buried inside me, believing that I was the only one hearing them.

Sometimes people would tell me that they were scared or intimidated by me, I would be shocked and confused! By me? Are you kidding? Can't you hear what I am thinking? If you knew the real me, you might think otherwise and run far away.

Understanding these thoughts and learning where they came from was the key to unlocking this part of me. The part buried in all those thoughts. The thoughts that created my reality. I once heard a speaker say, 'your brain is your supercomputer and your self-talk is its operating system''.

Man! Was I screwed. Where did this operating system come from and how could I upgrade my 'software'?

I grew up in the infamous Hamptons on the eastern end of Long Island, New York. A place where the rich and famous come to play. Big mansions, exotic cars, fancy parties filled with shiny people – you know the ones that seem to glitter and live perfect lives.

My childhood experience in the Hamptons was far from perfect. I moved 19 times in 21 years and never felt "home" anywhere.

My search for Home would start me out on a lifelong journey; to find family, to find inner peace… to find me.

So where to start?

Perhaps it began with the dad visiting my hospital roommate when I was just 14. She was there for appendicitis, me for swallowing 60 Acetaminophen in a failed attempt to stop the madness; stop the noise, and stop the pain.

When he visited his daughter, he would remind me 'God and the Universe don't make junk'. He would say it over and over again. He stayed by his daughter's side, and you could see the pain in his eyes as he watched her discomfort. I would have done anything for a dad like that. If I had one, would I have 'home'? As I did not have many visitors, in my mind I would imagine that he was visiting me too. But what did he mean, "God and the Universe don't make junk"?

On my release from the hospital, family therapy began. Week after week, a valiant attempt by my therapist to get me to talk, resulting in more untruths being told.

If I had been honest with her, it would have threatened the web of lies that had been constructed. Lies that were protecting me and those I lived with. No one could know the truth of what was happening. My lack of coping skills resulted in smoking and drinking, promiscuousness, violence, and rebelliousness. They became comfortable old friends, friends that I knew were very bad for me. But I could not quit.

'God don't make junk'. Oh, how this was haunting me. Couldn't he see what I saw? Didn't he know about my faulty software system? How could he see something in me I could not see in myself? I was no good and that just the way it was, the way it was always going to be.

Two years later, there I am standing in front of a judge in Family Court. My mom, who often struggled to find her voice, found the strength to place a PINS petition on me. PINS stands for Person in Need of Supervision.

There were times when she could not do anything but stare at the TV. But somehow, she went to court and took action. She was a single parent raising two girls and trying to keep it all going. She found the strength, in a last-ditch effort with me, to look to the judicial system for support. How very brave!

The judge sentenced me to over a hundred hours of community service warning me that if I did not do them, I would wind up in Juvenile Hall. As big, bad, and tough as I thought I was, juvenile hall scared the hell out of me. Deep down inside I knew if I went in, I was never coming out.

This was one of the darkest days I had ever faced. Remarkably it was the same day I was offered a light. To move me from the place where I fought everything good. A light that would guide me through this dark cave and lead me even when I was scared.

I moved from simply existing, just coping, to embracing my strengths. The strengths that came from the resilience muscle I had been developing. The strength to find and define my home.

The huge task of completing my community service hours in the time allotted was almost unachievable. My school guidance counsellor wanted to see me win. He saw more good in me than I saw in myself and arranged for me to do some of the hours in the high school office.

It amused me to be working in the principal's office. I had spent a lot of time there for getting caught smoking, drinking or some other violation of the Student Code of Conduct.

One day while I was working in the office, a woman called Jean Block came in. At the time she was President of the Parent-Teacher Association. She came from Georgia, south of New York and had a very sweet southern accent. She was graceful and kind and she seemed to genuinely care about others. Although I was always amazed by people like her, I was also very suspicious of them.

She approached me as I was placing mail in the teachers' boxes and if asked me politely if I would be able to hang up over 50 posters for a program called HUGS. I was not always very receptive to adults, especially when they wanted me to do something.

I stood there, in my torn jeans, (not a fashion statement, just worn out hand-me-downs), rocking a Metallica t-shirt. I had a chain that went to my wallet - no money in it, but I felt the need to chain it to me. My aim was to intimidate. To hide the fact that I was deathly afraid of you.

Something inside me guided me and I simply said, 'Of course Mrs. Block', and I set out with my tape and the posters.

I hung them up one by one. The posters were for a weekend-long leadership conference. Definitely not for me. That kind of thing was for the shiny kids. But as I hung each one, that inner guide seemed to be encouraging me to read a bit more.

The poster described the weekend conference as a place to go… let's stop there. I could get out of my house for the weekend! - that was enticing!

Then it talked about sharing ideas and opinions that were important to teens. I liked that, we were just talking about people, nothing that really mattered.

By the time I hung the last poster, the inner voice was so loud that it drowned out any resistance to the idea. That was it, I was going!

I went back to the office to see Mrs. Block. Immediately she suggested I sign up for the HUGS conference. And just like that, my eagerness to attend vanished out the door. An adult thought this was a good idea- it must be lame I thought.

Or maybe that was just fear rearing its ugly head.

FEAR has been explained to me as *Forget Everything and Run, False Evidence Appearing Real*, or perhaps *Face Everything and Rise!*

At that moment I wanted to run! She had the audacity to suggest I attend... a leadership conference! Did she not know who I was? Did she not know parents told their kids to not hang out with me? Did she not know I was failing? I fought her tooth and nail. Tried to stick to my story of being unworthy. A story I kept trying to tell. One, that if I am truly honest, I sometimes still try to tell today.

I told her my family could not afford it; she gave me the money.

I told her I had no way to get to Shelter Island (an island off of Long Island); she committed to finding me a ride.

I argued my mother would never let me go (this was a ridiculous argument as I think my mother secretly loved when I was out of the house); Mrs. Block called my mom.

Who was this woman and why was she more invested in me than I was in myself?

Every roadblock I built; Mrs. Block took down.

Reluctantly I went, determined to prove I did not fit in there.

It was a Friday evening and I walked into Willard Lodge. Although

I had never been to a camp, I expected this is what it would look and smell like. There I was, one of almost 100 teens. Shiny teens!

You know the type; 'ones the teachers always picked'. They were jumping in, introducing themselves to each other and seemed so comfortable in their own skin. Oh, how I fantasized about what that felt like.

I wanted to run and catch the first ferry home. But…In the very same nanosecond, I wanted to run, I knew I had found home.

The first question they asked me was to write 5 things I liked about myself.

Five? Were they kidding? That was the hardest question I had ever been asked. I could come up with 5 things I did not like with no effort at all.

Then it happened…I looked around and saw Sarah, the cheerleading star. Incredibly I saw that she was struggling to answer her 5.

Didn't she realize she was perfect?

Then I looked at Scott, the football captain and he was struggling to find his 5. What?? Everyone wanted to be him.

They were the shiny kids! But they were struggling right along with me to see the good that everyone else saw in them.

I had spent my life judging how I felt on the inside by how others appeared on the outside. I wanted to yell at them 'God and the Universe don't make junk!'

This moment remains as clear today as it was then, if not clearer. That was the weekend I discovered hope.

Hope that I could learn a new "operating system".

Hope that I could start to write my worthy story.

I began to work on myself in a very different way. I became resilient and found it reflected back to me from other people. I could see it in them, and I started to believe it could be true for me too.

In this space, I found my 5 truths and I found HOME!

I am now the Executive Director of the HUGS organization. We continue these powerful life-enhancing conferences multiple times a year.

Take a moment.

Write down 5 things that you like about yourself.

CHAPTER FOURTEEN

Do not dim your light, my dear, for anyone

Do not dim your light, my dear, for anyone. For when you show up, full of light, power, and strength, you are a force to be reckoned with.

Do not dim your light, my dear, for anyone. For when you stand tall, with your shoulders back, you are a leader.

Do not dim your light, my dear, for anyone. As the trauma that you have experienced, has birthed the amazing person that you are.

Do not dim your light, my dear, for anyone. For if they cannot love and accept you for who you are right here, right now, they are simply not the ones for you.

Do not dim your light, my dear, for anyone. For when you raise your hand in class, you demonstrate that you can ask the hard questions, while at the same time, provide the most thought-provoking answers to others.

Do not dim your light, my dear, for anyone. For when you say NO, you hold your power and do not cower in the presence of another.

Do not dim your light, my dear, for anyone. Especially when others are so determined on making you fit into the mold.

Do not dim your light, my dear, for anyone. Because every room you enter is an opportunity to shine your greatness upon all.

Do not dim your light, my dear, for anyone. Because just fitting in, is not what you are made for. You were born to stand out!

Do not dim your light, my dear, for anyone. For your male counterparts are never asked to do so.

Do not dim your light, my dear, for anyone. As so within, so without.

Do not dim your light, my dear, for anyone. For you are the I am, the Divine Goddess.

What would life look like, if you did not make yourself small, in order to make others feel good about themselves? What would life look like, if you allowed yourself to be fully expressed as you are, right here, right now? What can you accomplish when you live full out, shine full out, and be full out? You are unstoppable. For it starts in mind, and when you know that you are enough exactly as you are, right here, right now...you can. You can do anything! Achieve anything! Conquer anything!

I do not know the full extent of your dreams, visions, and destinies. But I do know that when you hold these in mind, know them in mind, and fully commit to them in mind, you will experience the life that you are looking for, right here, right now. For there is not a dream that is too much! Visions and destinies are meant to be bright and bold! There is truly only one YOU! No other human is like you, thinks like you, loves like you, is passionate like you! So, in this big, beautiful, creative life, live it fully! Show up first for yourself, commit to yourself and do not dim your light, my dear, for anyone.

I share these thoughts and mantras with you so that you know you can and will achieve anything you desire. As a strong desire, focused mind, and belief in yourself, is what will carry and support you in life. Others may walk paths with you, but you are the key to your own happiness, fulfillment, and achievement.

Do not dim your light my dear for anyone, for seeking validation outside of yourself will only leave you feeling frustrated, unworthy, and not enough. I am here writing and declaring to the world and universe that you are absolutely, positively, and divinely, enough! Yes, yes, yes!

Easier said than done, right?... to decide and know you are enough. Not really actually, if you train your brain, and allow yourself to know that you are enough at this stage in your life. You, my dear, are a beautiful, intelligent, vibrant teen girl. You are worthy of all the riches in the world and when it comes to value, there is no one like you that can hold a candle to you. There areis not enough gold, diamonds, or bitcoin to even put a value on to you.

Do not dim your light, my dear, for anyone. For when you shine and command your destiny, it is delivered ten-fold back to you.

Do not dim your light, my dear, for anyone. For as I write this, I am commanding the Universe for you, all the accolades and accomplishments that one can dream to experience in this lifetime.

Do not dim your light, my dear, for anyone. Even your family, because you know yourself best and what you are capable of and committed to.

Do not dim your light, my dear, for anyone. For if you learn this lesson, this masterclass, right here right now, you will put yourself in a position of authenticity, power, and love.

Do not dim your light, my dear, for anyone. For committing to yourself, and being bold and bright in thyself, is the most important commitment that a young woman can make.

Do not dim your light, my dear, for anyone. For when you do this, you show your younger sisters the way.

Do not dim your light, my dear, for anyone. As you will make those that came before and those that come after, so very proud to know you and be around you.

Do not dim your light, my dear, for anyone. For you are the most precious gift.

Do not dim your light, my dear, for anyone. You are meant for great things: abundance, prosperity, and success. It is your birthright!

Do not dim your light, my dear, for anyone. For if there is only one thought that I can leave you with, it is this: You are amazing! You are phenomenal! You are the best!

Now, what would life look like if before you went to bed every night, you thought about your light, and how can I shine and share my light even brighter tomorrow? How can I show up, fully expressed, in my full light, letting others put their sunglasses on if the brightness I exude is just too much for them? Remember, you are you, and you are divine, therefore, do not dim your light, my dear, for anyone.

Know that in this chapter, my goal is for you to know, do, be, and live. Know your bright, do your light, be your shine, and live your divine. I bet you are thinking, "is she ever going to stop? This seems very repetitive." And my answer to that is, no, I am not. Because you, my dear, are important to me. You are someone that I care very much about, and you are the exact person that I want to share my message with. Because the brighter you are, the brighter we all are.

Have you ever been around another that just shined? How did they make you feel? What strength did they provide to you? You too can be that shining light for others, but most importantly, for yourself. I am committing to you that when you show up, and glow up, and bright up, no one, not anyone can stand in your way.

Are you tired of this message yet?

Even if you are, I want you to read it again. I want you to read it, especially on those days where that light is not feeling so bright. Maybe when you have had a fight with a family member, girlfriend, or boyfriend. Maybe when you just wake up and you are not feeling it. Maybe after you lost that match, race, game, or competition. Or possibly when you lost that first love. You will have those days; it is a part of growth. However, you are not your thoughts, you are not your feelings, you are not the emotions that you are experiencing. You are a divine strong legend. And with that said, do not dim your light, my dear, for anyone.

Do not dim your light, my dear, for anyone. For you are a beauty to behold and one that dances on the most impressive stages in the land.

Do not dim your light, my dear, for anyone. For some day you will be in a college classroom, growing your knowledge base and competing for the top ranks.

Do not dim your light, my dear, for anyone. For your intuition is right about that girlfriend or boyfriend that you are in a relationship with, it is just not your jam, and that is ok.

Do not dim your light, my dear, for anyone. For you are the creator of your life, and I wish you to experience it to the fullest.

Do not dim your light, my dear, for anyone. For it is important to make a life for yourself, before you make a life with someone else.

Do not dim your light, my dear, for anyone. For when you contemplate a life partner, make sure they are just as bright. And just as important, they support and encourage you to shine even brighter.

Do not dim your light, my dear, for anyone. Some day you will be in the working world, a world that has been shaped by the boy's club, but do not forget you are destined to make your own way.

Do not dim your light, my dear, for anyone. For when you enter this working world know your worth, be your worth, command your worth, and earn your worth.

Do not dim your light, my dear, for anyone. For you are the future founder and Chief Executive Officer of your own Fortune 100 Company, reaffirming that the girl's club is just as expansive and powerful.

Do not dim your light, my dear, for anyone. As your creativity and ingenuity will lead others down a path, they did not think was even possible.

Do not dim your light, my dear, for anyone. As the position of Madame President is one that shines brightest throughout the free world.

Do not dim your light, my dear, for anyone. For whatever career path you take, make it full of divine strength, light, and you.

Do not dim your light, my dear, for anyone. For someday, you may have children, and they will need a powerful bright light to lead the way.

Do not dim your light, my dear, for anyone. Because children or not, every little girl in this world is deserving of seeing a woman that is divine, powerful, and confident in themselves.

Now that I have reaffirmed this message for you, is there anything left unsaid? Wait there is…

Do not dim your light, my dear, for anyone. For I am dedicated to seeing you live a full life. One that is in your perfection. One that is exactly amazing for you. A life that is full of potential with limitless possibilities.

Do not dim your life, my dear, for anyone. For your emotions create your beliefs, beliefs create your thoughts, and thoughts create your life. So let me reaffirm again, do not dim your light, my dear, for anyone. For you get only this one 3D life. You get this one ticket. You are the greatest and the most beautiful, intelligent, amazing, fantastic, gorgeous, vivacious, incredible person on this planet.

Do not dim your light, my dear, for anyone. The greatest gift that you can give yourself is to deeply and completely, love and accept yourself.

Say it with me, "I deeply and completely, love and accept myself. For when I do, I hold my power and show others that in the realm of relationship, I am most committed to myself."

Commit to your goals, dreams, values, and principles. You will not be disappointed in life, as you create into existence what you hold in mind, in heart, and in soul.

In closing, do not dim your light, my dear, for anyone. You are the I am! You are divine! And I love you very much!

CHAPTER FIFTEEN

Intuition

Intuition is the whisper of the soul - Jiddu Krishnamurti

Dear precious young lady,

I am so excited that you are reading this book. I truly share this chapter from my heart to yours. I wish that I had been mentored to follow my inner guidance, inner compass, inner knowing, and intuition. It would have saved me a lot of heartache. Take it from a woman who is a few years further along the road than you, the importance of LISTENING to all the wisdom and knowingness that you innately have inside of you. Learning to trust this place within you can literally save your life. Your intuition is hard wired into you. You do not have to do anything to acquire it; it is uniquely yours.

I have coached thousands of teen girls and you are not alone in trying to figure out how to hear, listen and trust what you feel is true for you on the inside. We all have this wise part inside us that whispers to us. It is where divinity resides, the wisdom and intelligence of the heart. It can appear as a deep knowing, without any evidence to support it. A gut feeling that you just know that you know; a feeling or voice of truth that reveals more than the five senses can tell you, hence why it is called the sixth sense.

You may ask yourself, 'how can I possibly know that'? You may be tempted to push the thought or feeling aside. I am inviting you to start listening to the inner wisdom and trust the truth that is coming to you from deep within. I give you permission to LISTEN; to trust and follow the biology of your body and the messages that it has for you. Your body knows. I also invite you to start listening to how your body gets your attention when it is trying to impart its deeper wisdom to you.

- Does your heart beat fast when you know something is not good for you?
- Do you feel a pang in your gut when something is off or wrong?
- Does your throat feel tight when you know that you need to use your voice to speak your truth?

These are some of the ways your body could be communicating to you; to warn you or remind you that you are out of alignment with what is in your best interest. Think of it like you have a best friend inside of you. Get to know her better. She will guide you and protect you as you grow through life.

Feelings in the body are directional signals and they have very important information for you. I want you know that you are strong enough to feel all of your feelings and encourage you not to be afraid of them. I encourage you to look at all your feelings with curiosity. Think of them like they are parts of you, and have important information for you. I tell my teens to pay attention to each feeling, write the feeling word down and put a circle around it. Then ask the feeling what it wants you to know and write what you hear all around the circled word.

This gives you some clarity around what is happening inside of you and will allow you to see what is coming up for you. Do this from a place of curiosity. Remember you are not your feelings. Do not let your feelings consume you, rather, let them inform you. Practice feeling your feelings. I often see teen girls and adult women who have shut off their feelings because they do not know how to process them; they are afraid to feel them. This leads to them feeling numb; not allowing them to feel anything bad, but nothing good either. They cut themselves off from their inner guidance.

Learning to process your feelings and emotions is key. 'Inner work' is required to being able to pause and discern where you are being guided. If you are in a position where you do not feel safe to feel your feelings or connect with that inner knowing, I encourage you to seek support from a trained professional. The inner feeling work is foundational for you to learn how to connect to, and stay in, inner alignment. This sets the groundwork for your external success.

Growing up, I had a strong sense of who I was supposed to be. But due to my conditioning, I quieted my inner voice to fit into my environment; to fit the mold of what was expected of me. To gain approval I trained myself to become more tuned into the needs of those around me, rather than my own needs. This put me in a vulnerable position. Little by little I ignored the wisdom of what my body was telling me and tried to be what others wanted me to be. When deep down I knew my body knew best.

It still amazes me today that when I was a teenager, I genuinely knew what was in my best interest, but I did not know how to honor my inner wisdom. I was not able to follow through with what was being revealed to me that no one else could see or validate. I was not nurtured to look within and honor my inner knowing and what I knew to be true for me. This caused me to second guess myself and I learned some valuable lessons through the pain of not being connected to my inner compass. I am telling you this, not for you to feel sorry for me, but for you to see that even if no one close to you or around you validate your truth, it still does not change the fact that it is your truth.

I am inviting you to start training yourself to LISTEN to all the wisdom within.

Here are some examples of ways that your inner knowing, inner guidance, and intuition can be diluted when you are more tuned into making others a priority over yourself.

- Quieting your inner voice out of fear of disappointing others
- Fear of rejection if you put forward your own ideas and suggestions in friendships and relationships.
- Giving parts of yourself away sexually when everything inside of you is saying NO.
- Not staying true to your values to fit in

- Being someone you are not, to keep other people happy.
- Not having the courage to honor your own voice and stay in toxic friendships and relationships because that is what is easier.

If you have experienced any of this, try this tool that I have given the teens that I work with: Close your eyes and put your hand over your heart and ask yourself the question that you want to know. If the feeling you get is peaceful and expansive then the answer is yes. If you get the feeling of tightness in your chest the answer is no. Practice this inward focus and connecting to the stillness and you will discover the answers within by how it feels in your body.

Awareness is the first step to being able to hear your inner guidance. LISTEN, LISTEN, LISTEN to what you hear. Trust it and follow the voice of your soul. I invite you to start on this journey and see how much fun it is to say yes to things you want to say yes to, and no to things you want to say no to. This helps you start to build that trust muscle of listening and following your inner guidance. Make it a daily practice to strengthen this inner part of your self. Flex this muscle daily by really tuning into how your body and feelings are trying to get your attention.

It is important that you remember that when you say no to someone, and they react in a way that is upsetting, it does not mean that you should have said yes. You are not responsible for how other people react to you honoring your inner truth and saying no.

Girls, love yourself enough to do what is good for you and act on what your intuition reveals to you. It takes courage, but you got this. Tap into that strength inside you; stand in your truth. Be true to yourself. I want you know that you are loved, you are more than enough, you are worthy, you matter, your voice matters and your truth matters.

The last thing from my heart I want to share with you is the invitation to think of your gut feelings as your guardian angels. The amount of wisdom and information that is available to you is so exciting! As you learn to access and trust this deep knowing place within; you will become empowered and strong on the inside. This will allow you to face people and situations with grace and love because you know that you do not have to justify what you know to be true for you. When you find this clarity on the inside, you will be guided more into your purpose, allowing your higher self to guide you to those paths in life that you are destined for.

LISTENING to all the inner guidance you have on the inside is one of the most exciting journeys you could ever go on. I hope you can feel the anticipation of all that can be yours as you step into trusting your own inner compass. It will guide you in your experiences throughout life. Wherever your intuition happens to lead you, wisdom will follow. All that you need is inside of you. I truly wish you all the best on your journey as you go through life.

Much Love
Teen girl Empowerment Coach
Renae Peterson B.N.

CHAPTER SIXTEEN

Creating healthy relationships

Hello Beautiful Goddess

I feel compelled to remind you how beautiful you are, not just on the outside, but on the inside as well. I know there are days where you may not feel gorgeous, but you truly are, through and through.

There are many reasons why I want to remind you of your beauty. Because when we are unaware of the beauty that lies within us or when we feel that we do not match up to other people's standards, then it becomes easier for us to allow unhealthy relationships into our lives.

Throughout your life, you will form many relationships. With family, friends, co-workers, or partners. In this chapter, I want to explore some of the things I have learned about how to maintain healthy relationships and avoid destructive or damaging ones.

At times you may find yourself allowing people to:

- push your boundaries
- attach in a way that does not feel good
- exhibit codependency issues
- be abusive

Any of these behaviors would be deemed as unhealthy.

I want you to understand the difference between a healthy relationship, and an unhealthy one. Sometimes it may feel like there is a gray area between these two forms of relationships but let me help you clearly define between the two. Then you will have a better idea as you navigate your journey through life.

Unhealthy Relationships

Unhealthy relationships will feel as though they are draining you.

You may find yourself questioning your actions or doing things that you instinctively feel are outside of your comfort zone. Maybe the other person in the relationship seems to be making a lot of demands on your time. Or they get upset when you are spending time with other people.

Unhealthy relationships can also be physically, mentally and/or emotionally abusive. Your friend or partner may show you what can feel like "love" most of the time but at other times they may be condescending, telling "jokes" which are very offensive or hurtful, criticizing you or getting angry about the smallest things. They may even act inappropriately sexually.

Healthy Relationships

Healthy relationships feel good! You get a great vibe from the other person or people and you just know that they genuinely want to see you win in life. That they will never judge you.

You will feel respected and valued in that relationship, believing that your voice matters. You feel able to make decisions without the other person criticizing you or making you feel bad. You will feel supported and able to speak your mind without fear of retaliation or abuse.

These types of relationships are also resonant, meaning that you feel excited and positive when you are around this person, unlike an unhealthy relationship which is dissonant, meaning that you feel negative emotions when you are around that person.

When I was a teenager, I would hear people talk about healthy and unhealthy relationships, but I was not sure exactly what that meant. For instance, a boyfriend wanting all of your attention seems cute until it becomes abusive in some way! I did experience this type of behavior in my teens.

Let's talk about a few scenarios and look at what healthy versus unhealthy behavior looks like in each one.

Dating

Your boyfriend says something hurtful and makes you feel bad.

You say to him, 'You know what? What you just said hurt my feelings.'

In a healthy relationship, he would reply "I didn't mean to hurt your feelings" and apologize. They would not make that comment again.

If the relationship is unhealthy, he may make you feel bad about feeling bad! They may continue to repeat their comment regardless of how it makes you feel.

Or your boyfriend is constantly flirting with other people. When you express to them that you do not like that behavior, a healthy person will apologize and stop, but an unhealthy person may gaslight★ you or make you feel as though you are overreacting and that they are not doing anything wrong.

★Gaslighting is a form of emotional abuse where the abuser convinces the victim that nothing they believe or remember is real.

Narcissists

Have you heard this term? Narcissists are people who have an inflated ego or are dishonest. They lack empathy or feelings. They have a hard time managing their emotions and typically are very negative. They exhibit abusive behavior towards others so that they can feel better about themselves, or so that they can achieve something that they want.

There is a range of narcissistic behaviors, such as:

- *Blame-shifting* - they do something wrong, but they put the blame on you as if it is your fault.

- *Isolation* where they try to remove you from your friends and family, other people close to you, from your job or even stop you from doing things that you enjoy so that your world revolves around them

This happens slowly over time. Any narcissistic behaviors are so subtle that you may not realize they are happening until you look up and see that you do not have any other relationships in your life other than the narcissist. This is what they want. They want to be the center of your world.

Narcissists also pretend to be the victim or act as though they are helping others hiding their true intentions from the world.

Compare this with what happens in a healthy relationship based on good communication and mutual respect. Disagreements will happen but you will both be able to get your points across without having to resort to offensive or disrespectful language. They will be able to see you speaking to someone without blowing a gasket and you will feel trusted in that relationship.

Finding Your Inner Goddess

There was one very important thing I did not learn until I was way past my teen years. I am so excited to share this with you now.

Do your best to love yourself a little more every day.

When you do this, you will find that you do not have room in your life to entertain or accept unhealthy relationship energy into your life.

Let me share with you a few ways that you can begin one of the most important relationships in the world which is your relationship with yourself.

First, find your inner goddess!

What is unique about you?

No two people are the same and that is what makes us so perfectly divine. It is not the things that make you fit into a crowd, but the things that make you stand out.

Learning to seek out those unique things about yourself will help you in your quest to learn to love everything about yourself.

Secondly, keep focused on your inner goddess. She provides you with the tools for healthy relationships, not only with others but also with yourself.

Third, find the things that make you happy. What are you passionate about? Some of the most beautiful relationships and friendships I have had have come from doing the things that I love and meeting people that have similar interests to me.

Creating Healthy Relationships

Now that you have an idea of how to find your inner goddess, and what healthy versus unhealthy relationships look like, let's talk about creating healthy relationships in your life.

I suggest looking at existing relationships in your life that do not feel good. You do not need an explanation as to WHY they don't feel good but listen to your Inner Goddess.

You may not like what she is telling you. But that voice is there for a reason. A guidance system for you. A system that will get stronger as you get older. You will realize the importance of it as you continue experiencing different relationships in your life.

Once you have established which of your relationships do not feel good or are dissonant, you can choose whether to remove those relationships from your life. Or if it is a family member or friend, you can establish boundaries that allow you to still be around them, or communicate with them, without accepting any unhealthy behavior.

It is important to understand that you have a CHOICE. Give yourself permission to surround yourself with only high value, high vibration relationships. Make a list of how you want to FEEL in the relationship that you have with your boyfriend, your family, or your friends. Do you want to feel happy when you are around them? Do you want to feel uplifted?

Write down those feelings, or even scenarios, to get an idea of what those relationships will feel like to you. It will help you to recognize when you know that a new relationship is the type you want in your life. And on the flip side, when you see unhealthy behavior, you can immediately detect it and make the choice not to allow that energy around you.

One of the most important relationships I have is with a very close friend who is an outlet for me. What is so special about this relationship is that there is no judgment. It is a safe place for me to express myself. She also gives healthy advice when warranted.

Having a similar relationship with someone in this way is great for when you need to get something off your chest. Or when you need a soundboard for ideas or stuff going on in your life. As you grow into a woman, having another perspective on situations, relationships, and other things is an important piece of cultivating your inner goddess.

I want to leave you with this piece of advice I was given by a loved one. She told me not to put my all into any single relationship because when you do that, you lose pieces of yourself along the way and once this happens, you will become a version of yourself that you think they want you to become versus you being your unique self and them loving you for who you really are.

Remember that you are divine, loved, beautiful, intellectual, unique, abundant, love in human form, a goddess. Perfectly imperfect. There is only one you and the people that you choose to have in your life will love you for you without trying to change you, put you down in any way, or be abusive in any form.

By reading this book, you are taking an important step in empowering yourself to be that fierce goddess that loves herself, and genuinely loves the relationships in her life.

You are one step closer to being unapologetically you, vibrating at such a high frequency that those with lower vibrational energy are detected by you in the blink of an eye!

You are learning how to protect yourself from unhealthy relationships in your life.

Here's to unleashing your inner goddess!

CHAPTER SEVENTEEN

Overwhelm

Defined as upset, to cover completely or submerge, and to overpower in thought or feeling.

And from experience, it can completely shut a person down.

When I was in high school, I was an over-achiever. I wanted perfect grades; to be a perfect gymnast and dancer; to fit in socially; and, of course, to have the perfect body. As I soon learned, life does not work like that.

All of my classes were advanced because learning came easily to me. I had a full schedule and tons of homework. I was competing with classmates over who had the highest grades.

I was a state champion gymnast transitioning my skills to become a dancer. I took lessons and practiced for hours after school, and more hours at home. Perfecting my skills. Choreographing, rehearsing, and performing. As much as I loved it, it was competing for my time and energy, with my academic studies.

On top of that, I was a teenager. Dealing with hormones and a body that was supposed to be changing into a young woman's but wasn't. Someone asked if I was a child prodigy because I still looked like I was 11. Fitting in and feeling 'normal' became difficult. My thoughts raced around being different and not being pretty enough.

So, there I was. Up to my neck in difficult classes, with my grades dropping, and feeling awkward in all of my dance costumes. I was overwhelmed! And once I hit that point, I froze. I had no idea how to think or feel. I did not know how to prioritize my time. I felt like

I was the only person in the world going through this. Soon I became depressed.

The problem was that I did not tell *anyone* how I was feeling, and I was not good at asking for help. As high school went on, I started to spend more time alone. Because I felt like no one would understand me. My self-talk became very dark. I felt buried under all the pressure of school, dance, and negative body image.

On the outside, it looked like I was a perfectly happy teenage girl.

This went on for years. Finally, in my second year at college, I hit a brick wall. I convinced myself I would never fit in; never be good enough. I did not deserve to be here.

I made the decision to end it by overdosing on a prescription medication. As you can guess, this was a complete shock to my parents. How could I have hidden all this from them for so long?

All because I felt overwhelmed by life.

That was my turning point.

Since then, I have spent my adult life making sure this does not happen to other teen girls.

My message to you is no matter how overwhelmed you feel with school, activities, social life, etc., remember. You are a light in this world. You are a Girl Goddess. You are pretty enough, and smart enough! You are worth it, and you deserve to live the life of your dreams.

So how do you handle being overwhelmed? Here are my tips:

School is a huge source of overwhelm. You ladies live in such different times. I am writing this in the middle of the pandemic, so as well as all the normal stress, many of you are dealing with a different school structure or learning online. On top of already challenging classes, you may not have all the support you feel you need.

Ask a teacher for help when you need it.

That is what they are there for. Teachers have a passion for teaching, and they love to see you succeed. You are not bothering anyone by asking for assistance. And special relationships with teachers are built by asking for their help. One of my son's teachers is still very special to us. She was his 'favorite teacher ever'. Because of the help he received from her. As he got older he visited her classroom often and even mentored her students.

Sports and activities are an important part of our lives. They teach us lessons and build relationships. Whether you are an athlete, artist, musician, or club president: it is good to have an activity that brings you joy outside of school. But they do take up time and energy. To avoid overwhelm, we need to figure out how best to balance school and activities. My advice: **Prioritize your time.**

Make a schedule. When you have a schedule, it is easier to have a clear vision of where you need to focus your efforts. Activities are scheduled around school, so block time before or after school (depending on your activity).

Most activities and sports require a couple of hours a day, which only leaves a few more hours for homework, family time etc. It is important to stick to your schedule! And if you do a seasonal sport that requires more time during that season, you might choose to make your school schedule a little lighter. It will make both so much more enjoyable.

Another place where we get overwhelmed is social media. As great as it to watch silly videos, or show the world your interests, it takes up a lot of our time and energy. We do not realize we have been scrolling for 30 minutes. That we have accomplished nothing. Even worse, we have spent that time comparing ourselves to people who have gone to great lengths to convince us that they are living a great life.

We can follow celebrities, get fun cooking, and craft ideas, laugh at silly pet videos, and even connect with like-minded groups. That is the upside of social media.

But there is a downside too. The declining mental health of our beautiful teen girls. Because they are bullied, or because they feel their life is not glamorous enough. The ping of constant notifications can be quite overwhelming. Remember, social media does not control you. ***Turn off the notifications!***

When you are on social media, *you* have the power to choose how much time you spend online; what you share; and what you browse. Block the people that may post negative posts or are argumentative.

Fill your feed with what brings you joy.

The last, and most important way to deal with overwhelm is self-care. Take special care of your mind, and your body, because you are special.

Eat healthily and eat enough to keep up your energy. You are a busy Goddess Girl who will thrive by eating nutritious foods. But don't forget to enjoy a treat here and there too!

If you find that you are short of time, and you are grabbing quick, unhealthy foods, think about planning ahead. Just as you schedule your activities; you can schedule your meals and snacks. This is not about what time you are eating, but prepping food ahead of time. If you take lunch to school, pack it the night before. Bring plenty of snacks that you can eat before sports or after school activities.

Most importantly, if possible, eat dinner with your family. It is about so much more than eating. It is connecting with those we love and sharing your day with them.

Journaling or freewriting is a very healthy way to relieve the stress due to overwhelm, and a great form of self-care. Journaling helps you sort out what happened during your day, what emotions came up, and how you handled things.

Freewriting is writing down whatever comes to mind at that moment. Random words, thoughts, and emotions will come out in your writing. It may be that nothing you write makes sense, but you will feel the release like a breath of fresh air.

Self-care can also consist of other things. Having a relaxing bath, a walk in nature, watching a funny program or listening to your favorite music. It is a short break from your daily hustle and bustle. And it reaps great rewards. Personally, I like to start my day with my self-care. I listen to guided meditations or meditation music for at least 10 minutes before I get out of bed. It clears my mind and leads me into my day with positive energy.

Overwhelm can happen before you know it. It can lead to negative thoughts and self-talk, feeling alone, anxiety and depression. But you have control. You have infinite amounts of Creator, Source, Divine, Goddess power within you.

Remember that. Hold on to that. Ask for help! Then, create a schedule that is balanced between school, activities, social media, friends, and family.

We are the creators of our lives!

A question for you: If you could create your ultimate schedule that brings you joy, what would that look like?

Go live your best life because you deserve it!

Love and light Girl Goddess

CHAPTER EIGHTEEN

How our brain works

Our brain is great at keeping us safe, and that is what it is designed to do however, that is not always what is best for us.

What if I could teach you some strategies to bio-hack your brain programming to keep your Big Emotions under wraps, would you want to hear them?

At the end of this chapter, I am going to leave you with 2 x 2 x 3.

2 x parts of your brain I want you to remember.

2 x parts of your nervous system and tips to recognise when one is activated.

3 x emotion regulation strategies that are going to enable you to perform your own Jedi mind tricks.

Warning: To explain this, I am going to need to geek out a little on the science.

Stay with me though, as it is super empowering to know how your body actually works. If I am about to geek out, I will give you a **SCIENCE ALERT** warning.

Brain Basics:

I would like to introduce you to the *Executive Brain* and the *Emotional Brain*.

Now before you tune out at the sound of the word 'executive' and assume this does not relate to you, this absolutely relates to every human on this planet and that IS you.

SCIENCE ALERT

The part of the brain just behind your forehead, which is known as the Prefrontal Cortex is the part of the brain that is responsible for your executive functions like planning, reasoning, recalling and good judgement. This is the part of the brain we want to be operating out of, the part that helps us focus in class; make sure we remember to pack everything for school and make the best decisions possible.

*We are going to refer to this as our **Executive Brain**.*

Deeper in the brain lies the limbic region, and we have two small almond-shaped parts of the brain called the amygdala.

This is where our big, emotive thoughts and feelings come from. This is also the part of the brain where what is known as the fight, flight, or freeze (FFF) response comes from.

Why does any of this matter? Well, those cheeky little amygdalae can hijack our body, our thoughts and our feelings. When they do, we may respond in a far more explosive and emotive way than we need to. This can lead to us getting in trouble at school or home, to having more fights with our friends and generally to make life much harder than it needs to be.

You know when something happens, and afterwards, you think about the event and cringe about what you said or did; and you wish you had a time machine to go back and undo it?

Yep! That's it! An *amygdala hijack*, the emotional brain literally takes over everything at that moment.

This is what we are going to refer to as our ***Emotional Brain***.

The brain's job is to keep us safe and therefore it is constantly checking the environment around us, looking for input. Recognising something that is either going to Reward us (can I get a high five!) or something potentially life-threatening to us (boo).

The brain is a bit of a negative nelly and is four times more likely to tag something as a threat. When our brain activates "hashtag threat", our FFF is triggered.

SCIENCE ALERT

When our FFF is triggered, the brain thinks we are in an actual life or death situation and prepares our body to respond. Blood is pumped away from the executive part of the brain. This leads to us losing access/connection to those executive functions we talked about. We literally cannot think straight. We are now operating from the emotional part of our brain. We probably get louder; yell more and feel like a volcano has erupted inside us. You know - that door slamming, yelling, screaming type of behaviour.

OK. This response is there to keep us safe right, that is a good thing yeah? Well yes. It is. However, the part of our brain that is wired for our safety has not evolved beyond its wiring in our caveman days.

This biological response, built in to keep us safe from sabre tooth tigers, now gets triggered in our day-to-day life. More importantly, we can turn this on just by our thoughts alone.

The kicker is that the teen brain is essentially still "under construction", with wiring and pruning of neurons occurring during the teenage years. The prefrontal cortex is not fully developed until the age of 25.

This simply means that as a teen you are more likely to drop into and function from your emotional brain. This can be hard work not only for you but for everyone around you!

Being aware of this and discovering some tips to help bio-hack your responses will help you find your way through what can otherwise be some drama-filled and very painful years!

FUN FACT

Brains are like fingerprints, meaning no two are the same and this means that everyone thinks, responds, and processes information differently. So, your friends and your parents are not always going to see things the same as you, as our brains are all unique!

SCIENCE ALERT

Let's deepen our understanding of what happens in the Nervous System, before moving onto the strategies we can use to bio-hack this whole primal response.

In our nervous system, we have what is called the Autonomic Nervous system. This is divided into two parts.

- *The parasympathetic nervous system: which is the rest and digest part of the body. This is our calm state.*
- *The sympathetic nervous system: which is what gets activated when we are in fight, flight, or freeze mode.*

Fight, flight, or freeze does not "look and feel" the same for everyone.

Fight response may be someone who always argues, whose voice is raised or who gets physically aggressive.

Flight response may be someone who walks away from a conversation or runs away when they feel under pressure or threat.

Freeze response may be someone who just shuts down and cannot get their words out. We think they may be ignoring us, or do not want to talk to us, but there is such a big traffic jam in their brain right now they simply cannot find the words they need to respond.

Naturally, we are meant to trigger our fight or flight, because it is there to keep us safe. However, we are also meant to be able to switch back into a rest and digest state.

It is possible to get 'locked' into the fight or flight state. You might recognise these people, they are the ones who are always jumpy, always on edge and who just cannot seem to chill out.

For me, years, and years of overactivation of my fight or flight system meant I often found it hard to relax or unwind, I was always angry at the world and generally just was not a very nice person to be around.

Let's pause and reflect. I want you to think about the last time your emotional brain (fight or flight) got triggered. Maybe your little brother or sister got into your room and stole something OR someone who you thought was a friend said something mean about you OR Mom or Dad said no when you asked to go out with your friends on the weekend. Whatever it was, think about that situation.

- What did it feel like in your body?
- Did you feel like a volcano had erupted inside of you?
- Did your heart race?
- Did your mind go blank, and you could not think straight?
- Did your stomach feel tight?

Those are all physical symptoms of fight or flight being activated.

Confused, fuzzy feeling = Blood rushing away from your executive brain.

Stomach tightness = the digestive system is turned off while blood is redirected to other parts of the body.

Heart racing = the release of stress hormones in your body.

Ok, we have spent quite a bit of time geeking out on science. That is because once we understand these responses in our body AND we can identify WHEN they are happening, we can call on strategies to help bring us back to both Executive brain and rest and digest.

So, to the Jedi mind tricks (biohacking) I mentioned earlier.

I am going to share with you, three emotion regulation strategies that will help you manage your big emotions.

These three strategies are labelling, reappraisal and curiosity.

Labelling

Labelling is simply giving a name to the emotion that you are feeling when you have a hijack. The more accurately you can name your emotion, the more effective it is in calming down the hijack response.

When you label your emotion a neurochemical process occurs in the brain and neurotransmitters release a cooling down effect. This is the start of bringing you back to a steady-state.

The next time you experience a hijack, pause, and try to identify the emotion you are feeling, is it anger, sadness, betrayal, hurt, annoyed. Get as descriptive and as accurate as you can.

Reappraisal

The second strategy is called reappraisal.

I like to think of this one as the "change the story you are telling yourself" strategy.

As human beings, we have the ability to turn on the threat response with our thoughts alone. This means we can simply think about a situation and: our heart starts beating faster, and our stomach feels like it is in knots. If we continue to think the same thoughts, we continue to trigger that fight or flight response in our body.

In the same way, if we can change the story that we are telling ourselves, from a negative one to a positive one, that dampening down neurochemical process in the brain can be activated and we start to come down from our hijack brain response.

For example; We send our friend a message and we have not heard back from them. They normally respond straight away so instantly we start to worry and think something is wrong. We begin thinking that they are annoyed at us, or mad at us over something that was said at school today. Then we tell ourselves the story "they are ignoring me". This all brings on a hijack and panic.

The longer we stay in that story, the more stress hormone is going to be released and we will stay out of connection with our Executive Brain.

A way to "reappraise" this or change the story we are telling ourselves is to notice that a hijack has been activated.

- First label it. I feel really ANGRY
- Then change the story to "she or he is probably out right now and left their phone at home, I know they will get in contact as soon as they have their phone again".

We do not truly know what has happened. Any number of things could have occurred that stopped our friend from being able to respond at that time.

But our thoughts and assumptions trigger that hijacked response in us.

Curiosity

Our third strategy is curiosity.

Studies have shown that when we are curious about something it lights up the reward networks of our brain. This means we physically cannot remain in that threat state when we are in a state of curiosity.

Let's go back to the example we used previously, about our friend who has not responded to our message. Once we have labelled it, we can ask ourselves what might have happened to our friend's phone.

Bio-hack Tip

Take long deep breaths while you are labelling, reappraising, and getting curious. The deep breaths trigger the blood to flow back to your stomach and also returns you to a sense of calm.

So now you know your 2 x 2 x 3.

The two parts of the brain are the *Executive Brain* and the *Emotional brain.*

When we have a hijack response our fight, flight, freeze system is activated.

Being able to recognise this response is a superpower because we can use this awareness to engage those emotion regulation strategies, *Labelling, Reappraisal* and *Curiosity* to bring us back into a rest and digest state and to return to our Rational Brain.

For me, these simple and effective strategies have been life changing. If I had known this as a teenager and in my 20's and 30's it would have prevented a lot of unnecessary mental anguish and pain. I have learned not to sweat the small stuff. To always look for the positive in any situation and to know that not everything in life is about me.

Get to grips with these strategies and you can live your life GODDESS-BRAIN-POWERED!

CHAPTER NINETEEN

Dream BIG, Believe BIG and Go for it

Stop the world! I want to get off!

Have you ever found yourself thinking 'they just don't get me'? Or 'I don't fit in'?

Have you watched life going on all around you, but thought that if they knew you, they would think you were crazy?

I mean, what is this messed up world we are living in? You just want it to stop so you can get off at the next stop.

By the age of 16, everyone thought I had messed up my life already and thought I was going to end up barefoot and pregnant! But I actually felt the sanest I had felt since I was 13.

Except for my excessive drinking and an eating disorder, I was feeling fan-tast-ico! Living in a bleak one-room flat and sharing a bathroom, but it was all mine and I thought it was a palace.

Oh, did I mention I had run away? Left my dad's home and left school. And that my wrists were healed from a couple of suicide attempts. Whoa... slow down you say...

Look. I am gonna share my story. Not just because I am still here... obviously I am, or I wouldn't be writing this! But because if you are struggling, I want you to know, that no matter who you are; what your circumstances are; what challenges you are facing; or what choices you have made in the past, you can have a pretty EPIC life. You can create a life you love and that excites you.

I am living proof!

I have travelled the world; lived in 3 different countries; climbed an active volcano and toasted marshmallows on flaming hot lava; flown a microlight plane through the Himalayas; been married (and divorced).

I have a healthy 18-year-old and live in Scotland with our hyperactive spaniel. We love the house we live in and there is a crazy story about how I bought it, without seeing it while on holiday, but maybe that tale is for another day.

I work empowering epic, magical, women to make changes and create impact on this world. I have also published 4 books before this one!

All of this sounds pretty impressive, doesn't it?

I am sharing to say "Hey! If I can have all this, and do all this, then so can you."

OK let me be clear about this. Your teen years can suck like a wet squid, and I would not go back and relive them.

But why don't we back up a wee bit here.

Take off those rose-coloured glasses and let me open my wounded heart to you. (Oh, yes! I love a bit of mellow drama, cue sad music)

My struggle began at birth. I was strangled by the umbilical cord on the way out; I was deaf, but no one figured this out until I was 5! How could no one notice...? I laugh about it now. I had a speech impediment because of the deafness, as I had learned to talk by lip reading and could not see the letter 'S' - so I went to 'cool, and it was 'unny.

3 operations and speech therapy got that sorted. But then I hit the 'trauma wall' when my idyllic happy family life exploded into World War 3 with a bloody divorce battle when I was 8. (I vowed I would *never* get married after that).

At the age of 14 I was anorexic. But I failed at that because I was hungry. Then I discovered bulimia. As a result of one girl innocently saying, 'I would rather be fat and happy like you, than thin and miserable'.

Whaaaaat? I was fat? (I wasn't).

I lost weight rapidly, but the compliments I received about my appearance just confirmed that I needed to 'be thin and look happy'.

Talk about adding fuel to the fire of false happiness and hidden depression.

I became the life and soul of the party from age 14, even though I felt 'soulless. At age 15, I attempted to cut my wrists a few times. Those scars are still visible. But there were emotional scars too. I lived in the darkness, suffocating in shame, wearing a mask painted with a hollow smile.

I was so freakin' angry. Picture a giant 2-year-old in a tantrum. But I only realised this when I stopped being angry. In all honesty, this only dawned on me in March 2021 Yep, I know this is recent. But hey! We are all a work in progress; all just trying to figure out our own hot mess.

We are about halfway through this chapter now, and you might be thinking; 'Whatever Iona, get to the point'. You might be rolling your eyes and saying 'You think that's bad? You don't know what bad is…'

I hear you. Whatever you are thinking you are right.

Remember, your viewpoint matters. You are worthy.

I am sure you are tired of adults saying that they know what is best. Or 'back in our day'; 'just get on with it'; 'just get over it'; 'just work hard'; 'just study hard'… blah blah blah

What if I said…

"Change the way you look at things, and the things you look at change."
- Wayne Dyer

It is all in our mindset.

We all look at the world through different glasses. Rose-tinted, bleak, broken, blinkered, tarnished - you see? The issue is not you; it is the lenses you are viewing the world through. Take the glasses off and we can then see ourselves, and our situations in a new light.

That is not to say that changing your view changes your immediate situation, but it can help you see clearly that you can make changes, and all change begins within you.

You come into this world magnificent and perfect just as you are. Then life happens and you start to learn how to 'BE'.

- By how you fit into your family dynamic.
- From your friends' perceptions.
- Learning how to blend in or stand out.
- Discovering what brings pain or approval.

Think of this as the computer programming of your mind. It happens at a subconscious level and determines how you interact and shapes your beliefs about yourself. Look at how simply my eating disorder started with a comment from a well-meaning friend; my attitude to marriage based on my parent's divorce.

These programs are running in the background. Even when you become aware of them and hit delete, they just move into the recycle bin. But they are still there. You need to empty the bin! Remove the blocks and rewire your mind.

Your mind, conscious and unconscious, is so amazing that you *can* rewire it. A trendy description for this is 'bio hacking'. It works by unwiring the behaviours we don't want and wiring in what we do want, using methods such as positive psychology, hypnotherapy, or repetition.

Now this is empowering!

You can make changes. *You* can adjust and choose your program. *You* can choose and create the life you want from the inside out.

Your mind is so powerful. It makes stuff up to fill in the blanks so that things make sense. Have you have ever seen an optical illusion? They are a great example of how your brain fills in the spaces to make sense of what you are looking at or feeling. But it can also fill in the spaces or show responses when there is no need to.

Notice what happens when you send a text or post on social media, and no one responds straight away, or there are no likes on your post. You might start 'catastrophising'. Thinking the worst. But maybe that person you texted was just busy. They saw your message and meant to reply and lost track of time. It is possible that they "ghosted" you, but if they did – you do not want people like that in your life.

We cannot change the people around us, but we can make small changes in who we choose to spend time with. By changing who we interact with; what books we read; what podcasts we listen to; which activities we pick; who we are following on social media; and who we look to for advice.

Changing our lives takes a little time but making the decision to make changes and improve our perception can happen in the blink of an eye. Things get easier and easier as we 'bio hack' our lives.

I could tell you that turning my life around was easy-peasy and that you can too. But it does require some effort. You can make changes to the BS, the limiting Belief System. You can change from within.

All the things I did. Bulimia, drinking, suicide attempts, were my attempts to change my world, from the outside in. I wanted to be seen, heard, understood. To have some sort of 'control' over my life. I was looking for external satisfaction and gratification, silently screaming for help. It took me years to uncover the secret.

The *only* person who could save me was me. It is like a huge cosmic joke!

We go looking for everything outside of us when all we need to do is pause and go within. I know this sounds like hippie-dippy stuff. It took me decades to finally figure this out.

My behaviours were all unconscious ways of coping and surviving. Of trying to make sense of this world and my place in it.

You are here to have an impact; you are a magnificent BE-ing.

You have a purpose, a mission that is as unique as you are.

In a recent talk at TEDx San Francisco, Mel Robbins, quirky self-help thinker, shared that scientists estimate the probability of your being born at about **one in 400 trillion**.

Think about that for a second!
You are unique!
You are one in 400 trillion.
That makes you a divine gift to this Universe.

Did you know you have around 60,000 thoughts per day and 95% of those thoughts are the same as the day before?

(1985, medical research conducted at the University of Maryland)

Be aware that YOU can choose how to think about your life.

Are the thoughts that you think empowering or disempowering?

This brings us back to your Belief Systems

Confidence
Worthiness
Relationships
Success
Health
Happiness

Your Limiting belief systems are all that hold you back.

Change your thoughts change your life.

Are you rolling your eyes because this all sounds too good to be true? Surely it cannot be that easy. The younger me would have felt that way.

I never said it would be easy, but if you can understand this now, you will be about 30 years ahead of me!

If I can accomplish what I have accomplished since learning this so late in my life, think what you can accomplish by learning it now.

Most of us struggle with identifying those beliefs. Are these familiar to you?

- Scared to be seen as different
- Worried what your friends will think
- Feeling unworthy
- Fear of failing
- No one will like me if I...

These are common 'limiting beliefs' that hold us back, stop us from taking risks and doing what we really want to do to create the life we want.

A quick share on 'taking risks' – did you know that your brain wants to keep you safe, and it is deep-rooted in our genes. Think back to the stone age when we lived in caves. Our brain figured that it was safer for us to stay safe in the cave rather than risk getting by a sabre tooth tiger if we left! I am simplifying here, but you get the idea.

Take that unworthy belief...

What would you do right now, if nothing stood in the way of the life you wanted?

You can start each day with the beliefs that you want to focus on, what do you choose to start with today?

You are not here to fit in, you are here to stand out.

Dream BIG, Believe BIG and Go for it.

I am not saying this will happen overnight, but you are capable of anything as long as you put your heart and mind into it

5 Quick tips to help you on your way:

1. Keep a future journal (not to be muddled up with a diary). This is for you to write down your dreams, soul goals, and gratitude. Write as if it has happened, in the present tense, not a faraway unobtainable dream, goal, or gratitude.
2. Write how grateful you are for all the amazing things that are part of your future goals as if they are part of your life right now. If life is feeling particularly tough, finding small things to be grateful for is like planting a seed, watering it and allowing it to grow. It will flourish and blossom.
3. Create a vision board for the life you will live, the woman you are becoming and the adventures you will have. You can do this on paper, or the computer. Choose images and words intuitively that grab your attention. Put a photo of you into the centre of the vision board.
4. This is the most important part. I want you to FEEL all this as if it is happening right NOW. FEEL it! You will begin to attract these feelings, visions and dreams.
5. Have FUN with all of this. You might have noticed that some of the adults around you are not much fun. Do not let this be you. Have fun, play and laugh every day of your precious and beautiful life.

ABOUT THE AUTHORS

Crystal D Life – Youth Empowerment Coach

Mother of three, Advocate for youth, published Author, Founder of It's A Girl Thing non-profit and Youth Empowerment Coach

www.empowerlifecoach.org

Natalie Smith – Life Coach

As we heal ourselves, our lineage, our children, and future generations all heal too! We are the ripple effect, my work starts the motion

www.nataliesmithcoaching.com

Carolyn Hobdey – Life Mentor

Carolyn is an author, life mentor and media commentator on imperative women's issues.

www.carolynhobdey.com

Michelina Cusano – Youth & Family Empowerment Coach

Michelina bridges the gap between parent and child, one child at a time, one family at a time, with love and compassion.

michelinacusano.com

Meg Scott – Youth Worker & Youth Substance Misuse Worker

A passionate youth worker with the hope to positively impact the lives of those around her through both her personal and professional experiences in this beautiful journey of life.

Laura Dempsey – Self-actualization Practitioner and Reiki Master

I am a Self-actualization Practitioner, Reiki Master and Author. I guide those who feel lost, to discover their true power within, heal trauma and reprogram their subconscious mind to live the life of their dreams.

www.true-transformative-healing.com

Eliana Keen – Self-Awareness & Emotional Literacy Mentor

I'm all about informing, inspiring, educating and empowering YOU to step into your true SELF!

http://www.arianarainbow.com/

Lesley Fraser – Empowerment Coach

Lesley Fraser is an empowerment coach helping women of all ages find their voice, follow their intuition and bounce back from life challenges.

www.mindfulmonkeys.co.uk

Hillary Sepulveda Brown – Spiritual Practitioner, Author, Speaker, E-RYT 500

Hillary journeys millions in recognizing that they are the ONE TRUE LOVE they have been searching for through subconscious mind reprogramming, & recovery of self by releasing Co-dependency

www.hillarysepulveda.com

Kim Garden – Intuitive Coach & Medium

I am an Intuitive Coach and Medium who helps women who feel unappreciated, burned out, and overwhelmed from putting the needs of others ahead of their own, rediscover their worth, voice, and true self at a soul level.

www.kimgarden.ca

Lisa King – Speaker, Author & Mentor

I am an intuitive, unconventional maverick who gifts others the ability to realise theirs, by enthusing them with their own beliefs of Self-Love and Self-Belief.

www.valentineking.co.uk

Judy Prokopiak – Master E4 Trauma, and Spiritual Psychology Coach

I guide female leaders and entrepreneurs over 40, to let go of the hidden stories of shame, self-blame and unworthiness, so they can fully embrace the truth of who they are and create their most remarkable "second acts"

www.Judyprokopiak.com

Kym Laube – Executive Director

Kym Laube is a well sought after speaker, trainer and consultant, specializing in mental health promotion, alcohol and other drug prevention, and leadership with an uncanny ability to speak with people and not at them.

Www.hugsinc.org

Mandy Monson – Wealth Empowerment Coach

I help women determine who are tired of the boy's club, determine their own destiny in the realm of career, wealth, and life.

www.mandymonson.com

Renae Peterson – Teen Girl Empowerment Coach

Renae is passionate about empowering teen girls lives and has been doing this work globally for 16 years Renae is passionate about empowering teen girls lives and has been doing this work globally for 16 years

www.beautifulinsideacademy.com

Tierra Womack, MBA – Confidence & Wealth Coach, Business Growth Specialist

Tierra helps successful female solopreneurs shift in their business to earn more while working less for greater time freedom & balance in their lives.

https://www.thebravewaytribe.com/

Randi Willhite – Biofeedback Practitioner and Spiritual Coach

Randi is an Intuitive Spiritual Coach who uses Biofeedback during her sessions to relieve stress, anxiety, pain and trauma; leaving the client feeling relaxed and on a path to finding their true joy in life.

www.wellnessgardenpath.com

Kathryn Van Der Steege – Mindset and Transformation Coach

Mindset and Transformation coach helping others transform their lives mentally, physically, emotionally and spiritually.

www.kathvdsmindset.com.au/

Iona Russell – Intuitive Mindset & Empowerment Coach

International author, motivational speaker, coach and radio host empowering women to integrate their uniqueness and embrace who they were born to be, living a life of fulfilment, freedom, and flow.

www.ionarussell.com

ABOUT SHE SPEAKS MEDIA

She Speaks Media are dedicated to creating resources that spark transformation in women and teen girls around the world.

Founded by Leanne MacDonald, a Spiritual Psychology Coach, New Thought Practitioner, Published Author, and Mum of Four.

She lives by the sea with her family, and her passion is to awaken women and teen girls around the world to their limitless potential, guiding them to consciously create their life.

Her passion was sparked by her own dark night of the soul, realising there was definitely more to life, and off she went on a journey of unravelling and recreating her entire life and identity.

She now leads projects guiding women and teen girls through their own journey of unravelling, healing their trauma, living in alignment with their true identity and learning to listen to their intuition and hearts desires.

www.theeverydaygoddessrevolution.com/shespeaksmedia
hello@shespeaks.media
pr@shespeaks.media

Beautiful Inside and Out Academy

Beautiful Inside Academy has been empowering and impacting the lives of teenage girls for the past 16 years.

Empowerment Coach Renae Peterson the director and founder started the Academy with a passion to have teen girls know their worth and own their power.

She recognized that In her teen years she wished she had been given the inner tools to know how to stay true to herself and to have the wisdom at younger age that women before her had gone through and had to learn the hard way.

She reflected that by not learning these skills at a younger age she had to unravel areas in her life to find her truth in her adult years.

Recognizing the importance for teens to have the opportunity to be coached and mentored to live their truth and have the inner tools to stay in this alignment she created the Beautiful Inside Academy.

Renae has dedicated her life and made it her mission to have teen girls be equipped with all the internal awareness and tools to be able to live with confidence and have the courage to pursue their dreams and step into their divine destiny. Beautiful Inside Academy has been empowering and impacting the lives of teenage girls for the past 16 years.

Empowerment Coach Renae Peterson the director and founder started the Academy with a passion to have teen girls know their worth and own their power.

She recognized that In her teen years she wished she had been given the inner tools to know how to stay true to herself and to have the wisdom at younger age that women before her had gone through and had to learn the hard way.

She reflected that by not learning these skills at a younger age she had to unravel areas in her life to find her truth in her adult years.

Recognizing the importance for teens to have the opportunity to be coached and mentored to live their truth and have the inner tools to stay in this alignment she created the Beautiful Inside Academy.

Renae has dedicated her life and made it her mission to have teen girls be equipped with all the internal awareness and tools to be able to live with confidence and have the courage to pursue their dreams and step into their divine destiny.

www.beautifulinsideacademy.com

For many high school girls and for many reasons 2020 was a year of loss and confusion, but for me I will always consider 2020 a year of clarity and gain. Because of Renae's Beautiful Inside Academy, I have truly gained confidence, self-value, warrior like mentality, and even my own queendom. Before Renae entered this chapter in my life I was really struggling to find myself and the beauty that already lied within me. You could definitely say I was having a typical identity crisis. At this time and for many years prior, I was fighting long and hard with myself by being a passive rescuer. I was introduced to the drama triangle, and it showed me where you stand in all of the drama and toxic situations in my life. Renae was able to show me the triangle ranges all the way from people that are rescuers and persecutors to victims. Up to this point in my life it was just me being soft spoken, would avoid confrontation, and especially lost my voice in any situation. Renae coached and showed me the way to breaking free from all that to be the most assertive mature queen that I am today. I have always had a hard time letting go of toxic and controlling people in my life. Having the mindset of being a rescuer always thought that my friends and others needed me and my mind loved feeding upon that recurring thought that I had to please them and be the people's pleasure all the time. Renae is an amazing mentor because she goes above and beyond as she goes along and takes the self-journey step by step with you. In my already busy schedule, Renae is the one that taught me that doing the heart work is the most important exercise you must have in your daily agenda. I would have trouble following what everyone says and being their little puppet of some sort and I wouldn't usually speak up. I really appreciate and love the homework Renae gave me one week. It was practicing the word NO. Saying no thank you, no not right now, no don't do that. Because I did the work, I can strongly say no to things that I don't fully agree with and know it's not what's best for me because I value myself way more. This was a great lesson that I have heard once or twice before and should have already known to use this skill, but I wouldn't ever do the heart work and with Renae I've learned to have the strength and courage to do it. I have said no to certain people in my life. Sometimes saying no can be really tough and painful, but as everyone knows, if you don't know pain, how can you experience the joy, and I am so grateful for that.

I have faithfully put in the time and heart work for the things Renae has coached me. I have learned how to forgive and trust, let people go who don't suit me, not to be anyone's puppet, as a queen I know what's best for me and know when the right time is to say no, and show up in every event being truly me and not putting on a mask. I am still developing the muscle and still practicing the beliefs and statements.

- Jessica Reeve

I was never good enough. Everything I did, I told myself I could have done it better. I should have gotten a better grade. I shouldn't have made that mistake. I would even tell myself something as simple as I should have been brave enough to say hi to an old friend. Living in a space where you're never good enough for yourself is so tiring and it ends up making you crash. It makes you start worrying about things that aren't in your control. I fell victim of trying to be the perfect human, and this resulted in terrifying panic attacks, beating myself up over every small thing that I didn't do perfect and never speaking up about serious topics because I wanted everyone to like me and for everyone to think that I am perfect. I quickly learnt that this is not how I wanted to live. I wanted to feel proud of myself and feel like I could achieve great things without the "If I did this instead, it would have been better" thoughts. After building up a lot of courage, I talked to my mom and told her that I need help, so I don't continue to put so much stress on my shoulders because the mental things I was going through was honestly too much for my body to handle. My mom immediately called Renae, and she changed my view on life forever. Ranae taught me how to organize my thoughts and be conscious of what I was thinking about so I could be able to recognize if what I was thinking of throughout the day was worth my time. It's quite simple, if the thought is negatively impacting me and it is not going to benefit me in anyway, then throw it away. I have been practicing this skill and this one alone has taken so much anxiety off me. I am now incredibly aware of what is worth my time to think about and what is just not worth my time. This has also helped me with my confidence around others. I decided to stop thinking of myself as an "outcast" or as someone that no one likes and instead, of someone who is worth other people's time and who doesn't need to listen to the negative things that people say to me. Ranae taught me that not everyone is going to like me, and it took me a very long time, but now I am okay with it. Because of these skills I am happier than I have ever been, and I know that I can feel all my emotions (positive and negative) and being able to feel them and work my way through them. If Renae didn't help me when she did, I honestly do not know where I would be in life right now, thank you Renae.

- Jena Nilsson

Having the tools and tricks that Renae taught me have been so helpful during difficult times. She taught me that your heart holds your identity, which is composed of who you believe you are. I was challenged to think about just what I believe in those internal places. In doing this, I identified many beliefs that were toxic and were essentially lies, which I unconsciously held close to my heart. During the academy, I was taught that "what we think about, we bring about". This means that our thoughts have such a big impact on how we act and what we do. The things we tell ourselves direct our paths. That's why, as Renae stressed, believing lies about yourself is so unhealthy. In a lot of cases, people don't even realize the lies they believe. Having a rude comment said to you or making a mistake can create a perfect opportunity for an unhealthy belief to form. The lies people make up about you cannot hurt you unless you let them, they cannot hurt you unless you truly believe them. Renae taught me an amazing trick to get rid of these lies. She told me to identify a lie I believed about myself and then say: "I am going to break agreement with the lie that I am_____ and I receive the truth that I am _____". This helped me rid myself of lies that were taking up room in my heart and be true to the real me. The first step to becoming yourself is identifying the lies you believe. My advice would be to try and analyse your actions. Some helpful questions to ask yourself could be: "Why did I react this way? What belief is fuelling my feelings of sadness or anger?" Becoming yourself can be a harder feat than expected; Renae has helped me so much with this essential process!

- Affia Zopula

That gut feeling! The feeling you get when something doesn't feel right, a warning, and sometimes an uncomfortable hunch. I call that my inner voice, inner guidance, or inner knowing. Your inner voice is there for a reason, it's an internal guidebook for life. It's a book that knows exactly what's good for you and what you need. Once you decide to take the path of listening to your inner voice it doesn't come right away, it's a lifelong journey to learn to understand it. It can also be like a muscle, the more you use it, the stronger it gets and the better you'll understand it. But you also need to remember that sometimes the good of listening to it won't come right away.

Your inner voice can save your life, or at least save you the suffering that you would have endured if you hadn't listened to it. My coach Renae taught me that before you can properly use it, you've got to love yourself. Everything starts with self-love. Loving yourself initiates trust in yourself, and when you get revelation from your inner voice you've got to love yourself enough to trust it. Trust it with your life, so that when you listen to it, you'll take action. Even when I was writing my chapter for this book, I finished my chapter, and it didn't sit right with me. So, I changed it, I rewrote it until it felt right. That was my inner voice telling me that what I wrote was not what I was meant to say, so I listened to my gut and redid it anyway! Recently, my wonderful coach Renae has helped me to connect to the importance of this feeling and being aware of it when it happens. It took me time to understand it, and that time cost me months and months of toxic friendships. I went through a hard toxic friendship, and I saw and felt red flags at the beginning. But what did I do? I ignored it. It took me a while to come to my senses and love myself enough again to listen. But even then, I struggled with the fear of not having a best friend anymore. The fear of her revealing the personal things I shared with her. The fear of making her life harder than it already was! I didn't know how to let go of the fear, but Renae helped me to decide to listen to what my gut was telling me all along and let go not only of fear but also of her. Renae helped me and so many other girls understand that you do not need to be available to let someone stay in your life who does not value you and keeps you from becoming the person you are meant/want to be. Especially when your gut is telling you otherwise! Don't let people remain in your life who don't prioritize you as an important person in theirs! You need to come first. This is not selfishness; this is selfless love for yourself. You can release people in love, you can do it with kindness, but you do not need to be everyone's best friend. Be true to yourself, follow that voice and feeling, and know that the body never lies! Trust your heart over your mind and let go of the fear! Honour yourself, listen to yourself, and love yourself. Connect to your higher true self, so that when you want something in life there is nothing and no one holding you back. Through working with Renae I learned all these important principles that are often overlooked in the world!

You were made for more! So, trust your gut because it's there to love you, and it loves you enough to tell you something is wrong. My coach Renae also taught me that I am in control of myself, and You are in control of you! Listen, listen, listen! Have the strength, love and tenacity to listen to your inner voice. Connect to your higher self and take the clarity of what your inner voice is telling you and run with it. Do not let the fear override your intuition. Trust yourself completely. Be true to yourself.

– Eden Haynes

Printed in Great Britain
by Amazon

70019985R10092